WITNESS

MISSIONAL DEVOTIONS FROM THE BOOK OF ACTS

Darren Carlson

New Growth Press, Greensboro, NC 27401
newgrowthpress.com

Cover Design: Faceout Studio, faceoutstudio.com
Interior Typesetting and Ebook: Lisa Parnell, lparnellbookservices.com

ISBN: 978–1-64507–563–9 (paperback)
ISBN: 978–1-64507–564–6 (ebook)

Library of Congress Cataloging-in-Publication Data on file

Printed in Colombia

29 28 27 26 25 1 2 3 4 5

For my children,

Makena, Gianna, Dakota, Josiah, and Sierra

"No one encourages me more than Darren Carlson when he tells stories from the front lines of the global church. I just love the way this devotional bridges between Acts and today to show how God still works in miraculous ways."

Collin Hansen, Vice President for Content, The Gospel Coalition; host of the *Gospelbound* podcast

"This is a unique and delightful blend of biblical insight and snapshots of what is happening in and through the church around the world. A wonderful way to enrich and enlarge our vision of what the message of Jesus can accomplish."

Sam Allberry, Immanuel Nashville; author of *One with My Lord*

"How would your family's perspective on God's work in the world change if you heard reliable reports of his work among the nations? This book relays faith-building stories of current events and connects them to biblical teaching about the work Jesus did right after he ascended to heaven. We've already started reading it with our kids, and our hearts have been stirred!"

Dave and Gloria Furman, Chancellor, Gulf Theological Seminary; author of *Embracing God in Your Suffering*; author of *Missional Motherhood*

"With reflections on Acts and anecdotes from the global church, Darren Carlson invites us to consider how the gospel changes lives—and could change us. Within a generation, the apostles' witness turned the world upside down. Reading this might turn us right-side up."

Elliot Clark, Author of *Evangelism as Exiles* and *Mission Affirmed*

"There are few prayers God delights in answering more than, 'Use me to make your name known.' *Witness* connects God's faithfulness in the early church with his faithfulness in building his church today in a way that will fuel your faith to praise, pray, and trust God in fulfilling the Great Commission."

Garrett Kell, Pastor, Del Ray Baptist Church

"Want to see Acts with new eyes, learn more about global Christianity, and ponder in prayer God's place for you in the amazing work he is doing worldwide? Then this book is for you. Let your life and voice join in with the dramatic expansion of Christ's saving work in the current generation."

Robert W. Yarbrough, Professor of New Testament, Covenant Theological Seminary

"Carlson writes, 'We are living in what may be the greatest advance of the gospel in history.' But the continuing task is also more vast than any prior time. I pray that Carlson's delightful missiological exposition of Acts and the encouraging examples he gives will be used by the Lord to light a fire for missions in the global church."

James E. Plueddemann, Retired professor of missions, Trinity Evangelical Divinity School; former chair of educational ministries, Wheaton College; former International Director, SIM

"Carlson's book is an encouraging and hopeful call to pray to the Lord of the harvest, to watch for his saving power among the nations, and to continue in the Great Commission. This book rightly directs all our hope to God alone, who builds his church through imperfect servants."

E. D. Burns, Professor, Asia Biblical Theological Seminary; executive director of training and development, ABWE; missionary in Southeast Asia

"This engaging devotional volume by Darren Carlson combines solid, insightful exposition of the book of Acts with sparkling, inspiring stories of the contemporary worldwide church. It's a blast of fresh air, a spotlight shining on our global God. Read this book to be more amazed by who God is and to be more attuned to what he's doing among the nations."

Stephen Witmer, Lead Pastor, Pepperell Christian Fellowship; author of *A Big Gospel in Small Places* and *Eternity Changes Everything*

"We often forget that the New Testament was written in a missionary context, and the book of Acts is a missionary book. I love how *Witness* takes the truths of God's Word and connects them in a powerfully practical way with the work God is doing around the world today."

Scott Dunford, Pastor, Western Hills Church; cohost, *The Missions Podcast*

CONTENTS

INTRODUCTION

WE ARE living in what may be the greatest advance of the gospel in history. More people than ever, in more corners of the world and in more languages than ever, are worshipping the Lord and following Jesus. The Holy Spirit is moving in ways that are hard to even explain. However, our perception of the Lord's work around the world often remains limited, as we struggle to grasp the full extent of what God is doing in both our neighborhoods and far-flung locations. We live busy lives and have pressing concerns—this doesn't leave a lot of room for investigation. Not only that, but much of what happens goes unreported. We don't have regular streams of information to know about spiritual revival across town—let alone across the world. Combined with our tendency to forget what God has done—even in our own lives—it's no wonder that discouragement, fueled by our limited knowledge of what is happening, can easily set in.

I've seen firsthand what the Lord is doing, and I can't wait to share it with you. I've spent years teaching the Bible around the world and equipping pastors and church leaders from a myriad of countries. I've invested countless hours researching and documenting the story of how the Lord is drawing people to himself and growing his global church. My heart is to take you on a trip around the world—a virtual tour of God's work in people groups both near and far—so you can see and marvel at what God is doing right now. I want to anchor these stories in the story of the early church in Acts so that you can see that the same God who turned the world upside down two thousand years ago is still changing lives and communities today. As you consider his work in the first century, my prayer is that you will consider what he wants to do in and through you—and in and through his church—right now.

I want to remind you that even now, God is orchestrating innumerable stories that remain unknown to us. Although these individual narratives may not be transformative on their own, we have been gifted with Scripture that possesses the power to nurture, nourish, and ultimately transform our lives. I invite you to join me in a journey through the book of Acts, which beautifully captures the growth of the early church from a small group of Jewish believers in Jerusalem to a diverse and extensive movement that spanned the first-century Roman world. My goal is to demonstrate that the same God who was active in the book of Acts continues to work in our lives today—breaking new ground and expanding his kingdom.

As you move your way through this devotional, I encourage you to dedicate the next sixty days to praying for the global church. Consider also utilizing resources such as the *Operation World* app, which guides users in praying for a different country nearly every day of the year.

Above all, these devotions are designed to deepen your relationship with God and broaden your understanding and expectations of what he does around the world. It is my sincere desire that, as you engage with the beauty of Christ as portrayed in the book of Acts, your appreciation and love for him and his gospel will grow even stronger.

DAY 1

THE MINISTRY OF JESUS CONTINUES

ACTS 1:1–3

In my former book, Theophilus, I wrote about
all that Jesus began to do and to teach until the day
he was taken up to heaven, after giving instructions
through the Holy Spirit to the apostles he had chosen.
After his suffering, he presented himself to them and gave
many convincing proofs that he was alive.
He appeared to them over a period of forty days
and spoke about the kingdom of God.

WHY READ the book of Acts?

Acts was written to give a detailed account of the promises fulfilled in Jesus Christ so that we can have full confidence in his ongoing life and work. Both the Gospel of Luke and the book of Acts serve this apologetic purpose: They emphasize eyewitness testimony as the bedrock of historical credibility for the Christian faith. In their introductions, Luke (who wrote both books) stresses that these are not fabricated legends but are thoroughly investigated accounts, founded on real events and real people. He carried out extensive field research, meeting and interviewing those who had encountered Jesus personally to ensure that his narrative would be trustworthy.

If you were asked where Jesus is now and what he's doing, how would you respond? Many Christians find the ascension puzzling, unsure how it applies to everyday life. Yet the book of Acts is all about the continued ministry of the ascended Jesus. It stands out among New Testament writings and was penned by Luke, the traveling companion of Paul—and the only known Gentile writer of a New Testament book.

Luke and Acts share a common purpose: they're both addressed to Theophilus, likely a Gentile, to explain how Jesus relates to his followers. Luke covers "all that Jesus began to do and teach," while Acts depicts how Jesus continues to work in the growth and development of the early church. Jesus doesn't stop teaching at the end of the Gospels or when he ascends. He simply shifts his mode of ministry.

Some claim that the Gospel of Luke focuses on Jesus and the book of Acts focuses on the church. But Luke won't let us think that way. Together, they reveal one continuous story: Luke shows the earthly ministry of Jesus, and Acts shows his heavenly ministry. Though he's no longer physically present, he still teaches and works through the Holy Spirit. That same Spirit empowers the apostles to proclaim the risen Messiah and instruct new believers. Missionaries, pastors, and teachers have passed on these truths century after century across the globe.

A key term here is *ascension*. It points to a change in the way Jesus relates to us. You may recall these words from the Apostles' Creed:

> [He] suffered under Pontius Pilate, was crucified, died, and was buried . . . on the third day he rose again; he ascended into heaven, and sits at the right hand of God the Father almighty.

The ascension isn't just a historical marker; it's a present reality. Jesus reigns from heaven right now, overseeing the spread of his kingdom by the Spirit's power.

In what ways have you seen Jesus continue his ministry through the Holy Spirit in your life or in the lives of those around you? Take a moment to recognize where God is at work and how you might join in with renewed purpose and hope.

The Acts of Jesus Continue Today

In my PhD research, I met ministry workers who were stretched thin and discouraged, uncertain about God's work in their own city. One group found Iranians responsive to the gospel but Afghans indifferent; another group just a mile away had the opposite experience. Each ministry formed plans based on limited vantage points, success, and disappointments.

We can all slip into tunnel vision, focusing on what's right in front of us and missing God's bigger picture. Yet Jesus has been at work through the Spirit since his ascension—and he continues to be. We often fail to see the breadth of his activity. I like to remind myself that God is doing thousands of things throughout the world and in my life—I'm aware of five, and I misinterpret three.

Let's keep our eyes open for God's hand in unexpected places. When we grasp the ongoing work of Jesus through his Spirit, we find fresh encouragement and clarity for our own roles in the story. We are part of something vast—spanning centuries and continents, resting under the sovereign care of our ascended Lord.

Reflection

Take a moment to pray that God might open your eyes to what he is doing both around the world and around you so that you can join in his work.

DAY 2

YOU WILL BE MY WITNESSES

ACTS 1:7–8

He said to them: "It is not for you to know the times or dates the Father has set by his own authority. But you will receive power when the Holy Spirit comes on you; and you will be my witnesses in Jerusalem, and in all Judea and Samaria, and to the ends of the earth."

WHAT IS said last matters most.

Jesus's final words before ascending to heaven confounded his followers, who were expecting a political restoration of Israel. Instead, Jesus spoke of a kingdom spread not through political maneuvers but by Spirit-empowered witnesses—a call the church has often struggled to embrace.

Jesus wanted his disciples to focus not on the date of his return but on the mission he gave them. The time between his ascension and his return would be marked by the power of the Holy Spirit infusing the lives of believers so that a watching world would see and have an opportunity to respond to the gospel. Paul highlights this reality in his first letter to the Thessalonians: "Our gospel came to you not simply with words but also with power, with the Holy Spirit and deep conviction" (1:5).

In Isaiah 43:10–12, we see that God's people are called to show the nations that he alone is God. In the book of Acts, we see that while the apostles are the first witnesses, others also share their testimony and display transformed lives, bearing witness in both word and action.

If we fail to see ourselves as Christ's witnesses, we lose a core part of discipleship. Evangelism should flow naturally from our identity as beloved sons and daughters of God—sons and daughters who can't wait to share what God has done for them.

Empowered by the Holy Spirit, the early Christians took the good news from Jerusalem to Judea and Samaria (Acts 8–12) and then "to the ends of the earth" (Acts 13–28). This same mission stretches on today, calling us to make disciples everywhere.

We are witnesses, empowered by the Holy Spirit to bear witness to Christ. So, let us dethrone fear and enthrone Christ as Lord over our lips and our lives. Have you experienced the Holy Spirit's power to share the good news of Jesus with others? Are you living in a way that proclaims the glory and transforming grace of our Lord?

The Expansion Through Witnesses

In the last century, we have witnessed an unprecedented expansion of the Christian faith, often through unlikely people and circumstances.

In 2008, Ahmad, an Afghan refugee, fled to Iran. He later moved to Turkey, where he became a Christian. From there, he traveled to Greece and then Norway, seeking asylum. His request was denied, so he went to Germany, where he joined a local congregation and was baptized. After his asylum application was rejected again, he returned to Norway, but officials couldn't determine his country of origin.

In an astounding turn of events, Ahmad responded to this setback by requesting deportation back to Afghanistan. The Lord had impressed upon his heart the urgency of sharing the gospel with his fellow countrymen. Upon his return, he started an underground church. Sometime later, a South African Bible teacher of this church was tragically killed by the Taliban. Ahmad fled to India, where he was able to finish college, and eventually returned to Europe, where he was granted asylum. Today he serves in an international congregation.

Through all the trials and hardships, no matter where the Lord placed him, his commitment remained the same—to bear witness for Jesus.

Reflection

No matter where life takes you, you've been given power through the Holy Spirit to bear witness to the resurrected Christ. Do you see yourself as a witness? Who in your life could you talk with today about Jesus?

DAY 3

WAITING ON THE LORD

ACTS 1:9–11; 2:1

After he said this, he was taken up before their very eyes,
and a cloud hid him from their sight. They were looking
intently up into the sky as he was going, when suddenly
two men dressed in white stood beside them.
"Men of Galilee," they said, "why do you stand here
looking into the sky? This same Jesus, who has been taken
from you into heaven, will come back in the same way
you have seen him go into heaven."

When the day of Pentecost came,
they were all together in one place.

I LOVE how the story of the ascension unfolds. Jesus rises into heaven, and the disciples are left staring up at the sky. Suddenly, angels appear (as though it's nothing unusual) and ask, "Why are you standing here?" The disciples had just seen Jesus depart in a miraculous way, so they were understandably awestruck. Yet they had missed what he told them to do: return to Jerusalem and wait for the Holy Spirit. Instead of obeying immediately, they lingered. The angels gently rebuked them: "What are you doing?"

Eventually, the disciples headed back to Jerusalem. How long did they wait? About ten days. We often forget that they had no idea how long this would last. Ten days is a long time when you don't know what's coming next.

Pentecost literally means "fiftieth day." It's the Greek name for the Jewish Festival of Weeks, marking the end of the grain harvest (Leviticus 23:15–16). The Israelites were to celebrate by bringing bread from new grain as a firstfruits offering. But Acts 2 highlights a new kind of "harvest." Instead of bread, three thousand souls are brought into the kingdom of God in this miraculous event.

Jewish tradition also taught that fifty days after the original Passover, Moses received the law on Mount Sinai. Thus, by the first century, Pentecost carried multiple layers of meaning. It drew travelers from across the Roman Empire, with some estimating that as many as a million people converged on Jerusalem during Pentecost. With roads dry and travel easier in June, God chose the perfect moment to reveal something remarkable.

Acts 2:1 says, "they were all together in one place." This likely included not just the Twelve, but a larger group of about 120 believers, possibly in an open-air space near the temple. They must have felt abandoned twice in a very short time: First, they lost Jesus to death, only to see him resurrected; then he ascended to the Father, leaving them to wait again. But they didn't wait passively. Acts 1 shows the believers praying and staying unified. God was at work in their waiting. Then, like a rushing wind, the Holy Spirit arrived.

When was a time you had to actively wait on the Lord? What did you do?

I've Been Waiting for You

A missionary I know was serving among Muslims in a remote region. One evening, a woman came to her with a child who had been severely burned. The missionary began tending to the child's wounds, explaining to the mother, "I'm doing this in the name of Jesus, who loves you." After a few minutes of conversation, the

Muslim woman smiled and said, "Oh, that's who he is! I've been waiting for you."

This woman had grown up in folk Islam. When she was fourteen years old, she was given as a bride to a witch doctor who was thirty years her senior. She was given as payment because the witch doctor had placed a curse on her father's neighbor for planting crops on their land. The curse worked—the neighbor's eldest son dropped dead.

Not long after her marriage, the young woman had a vision. A man, dressed in white and shining like the sun, appeared to her. He told her, "I am the way, the truth, and the life. Follow me." She explained, "He showed me the scars on his hands and feet and told me he was God. He promised that one day he would rescue me and that someone would come to tell me his name."

Turning to the missionary, the woman said, "I've been patiently waiting for you."

Reflection

Even in our seasons of "not yet," God is powerfully at work, preparing us to witness a greater harvest than we imagined—just as he did for the disciples waiting for Pentecost. The same Savior who once seemed absent has a plan to reveal himself in ways we don't expect, often right at the moment we feel most abandoned or uncertain. Where is God asking you to wait on him, and how might he be inviting you to actively trust and serve during that wait?

DAY 4

GOD SPEAKS MY LANGUAGE

ACTS 2:6–16

When they heard this sound, a crowd came together in bewilderment, because each one heard their own language being spoken. Utterly amazed, they asked: "Aren't all these who are speaking Galileans? Then how is it that each of us hears them in our native language?" (2:6–8)

AT PENTECOST, the Holy Spirit descends with overwhelming power, and the disciples are astonished. They hear a mighty rushing wind, and something like tongues of fire appear over their heads. Immediately, the disciples leave the room where they were gathered and step into the crowds.

The city of Jerusalem is packed due to the feast, with people from all over the known world. Most of them would have spoken Greek as a common language, but as the Christians begin speaking to the multitudes, they astonishingly don't speak in one language. Instead, they spontaneously declare the wonders of God in a multitude of languages. "We hear them declaring the wonders of God in our own tongues," the crowd says in astonishment (2:11).

The responses from the crowd are exactly what we might expect. Some are "utterly amazed," while others are "amazed and perplexed" (2:7, 12). Still, others dismiss the scene, attributing it to drunkenness. But they are wrong. Peter stands up to clarify they are not drunk but filled with the Holy Spirit, fulfilling the ancient promises of Joel 2 before their very eyes.

There is so much in this story to unpack, but I want to focus on one aspect. If you are familiar with the Bible, one passage that might come to mind is the Tower of Babel in Genesis 11. Acts 2 is, in a sense, a reversal of Babel. In Genesis 11, humanity is united in its rebellion, attempting to build a tower to make a name for themselves. In response, God confuses their language and scatters them. The diversity of languages is presented as a form of judgment.

In Acts 2, we see a dramatic reversal of the curse at Babel: instead of languages causing confusion and division, the Holy Spirit makes the gospel accessible to everyone present in their own tongue. Linguistic barriers are broken, and a new unity emerges—one that transcends the differences of language that separated people. This moment foreshadows the future reality pictured in Revelation 7, where believers from every tribe, language, people, and nation gather in worship. Our unique cultural identities remain, but rather than dividing us, they now contribute to the beautiful tapestry of God's redeemed family.

The Holy Spirit could have easily empowered the early Christians to preach only in Greek, a language most of the people in Jerusalem would have understood. But from the very beginning, the Christian faith was not limited to one language or culture. It was meant for all people, in all their diversity. Here we see the Father's heart for removing all barriers to the gospel—not by removing the diversity of expression, but by making the good news accessible to people just as they are.

Does God Speak My Language?

The explosive spread of Christianity around the world has been largely driven by the translation of Scripture into the vernacular languages of countless people groups. This has given birth to churches and movements that no longer need to rely on a dominant language like English or French. Wycliffe Bible Translators, founded by Cameron Townsend, has played a critical role in this work. In

1919, Townsend was challenged by a Guatemalan Indian who asked him, "If your God is so smart, why doesn't he speak my language?" Taking up the challenge, Townsend spent ten years translating the New Testament into the Cakchiquel language. Today, the Bible has been translated in full into 756 languages, with at least some portion of Scripture available in 3,756 languages.

Today, there are still over 3,400 languages without any portion of the Bible translated.[1]

Reflection

What would it be like if the Bible were not translated into a language you know? What kind of impact would it have on your church? Take a moment to pray for all the people involved in Bible translation. Go online to learn about the work of some of these ministries and what it takes to make Scripture available to people in their heart languages.

DAY 5

A NEW ALLEGIANCE

ACTS 2:37–38

When the people heard this, they were cut to the heart and said to Peter and the other apostles, "Brothers, what shall we do?" Peter replied, "Repent and be baptized, every one of you, in the name of Jesus Christ for the forgiveness of your sins. And you will receive the gift of the Holy Spirit."

IN THE first century, baptism was a practice well known in religious circles. The Jews used it as a symbol of cleansing or being washed of sin. They would require Gentile converts to be baptized in a ceremony to remove ceremonial uncleanness. It was also a rite of initiation into a group. Jews also used baptism via immersion as an act of repentance. That was John the Baptist's message as seen in passages like Mark 1 and Luke 3: repent and be baptized. John's baptism was "a baptism of repentance for the forgiveness of sins." (Mark 1:4)

Because Jews regarded baptism as something necessary for the cleansing of Gentile converts, the idea of a Jewish person needing to submit to baptism would have been unthinkable. They didn't need to be ceremonially clean. They didn't need to be initiated into the family of God. They were God's people! But as for three thousand people on the day of Pentecost (many of them Jews), they chose to submit to Peter's teaching and break away from their own identities in this radical step. That morning there had been 120 believers, and by the time everyone went to bed that night, thousands of people had been baptized in the name of Jesus in the pools in Jerusalem. What a sight that must have been!

Baptism is like putting on team colors, and these Jews were announcing that they were switching teams. It was like putting a ring on their finger on their wedding day. It didn't create the marriage, but it was a sign that a marriage had taken place.

I'm going to leave behind the debate among Christians about baptism. Wherever you land on this issue, there is no category for an unbaptized Christian. Baptism is so closely tied to conversion that Peter expects these Jews to be baptized immediately. One passage that highlights how closely baptism is tied to becoming a Christian is found in Acts 8. Philip runs into an Ethiopian who is reading Isaiah. These words are then recorded:

> Then Philip began with that very passage of Scripture and told him the good news about Jesus. As they traveled along the road, they came to some water and the eunuch said, "Look, here is water. What can stand in the way of my being baptized?" (8:35–36)

How important was baptism in the sharing of the gospel? Think about this. Philip tells the eunuch the good news of Jesus, and his immediate response is an understanding of the next step of obedience: baptism.

If you have not been baptized, what is holding you back? Likewise, if you have believing friends who are not baptized, pray for an opportunity to encourage them to obey Christ's command.

When Am I Getting Baptized?

My friend Mihalis has spent a lot of time ministering to Muslims and has baptized many of them in a water fountain in front of the ministry center where he works. One of the Muslims he got to know was a Kurdish man from Syria. He had been injured and broken his arm and leg, so Mihalis would take him to the hospital every week for rehab. During one of those rides, this Syrian became a Christian. He lived in a refugee camp, and every week he would distribute New Testaments in Arabic. After some time, he came and said, "I want to get baptized." Mihalis encouraged him to finish his discipleship program, and then they would do that.

This conversation happened on a Sunday night. The next Friday, during the night, at around 2:00 a.m., the new Christian was attacked because his neighbors were tired of him talking about Jesus. The young man survived the fight, but Mihalis took him out of the camp to stay somewhere safe. When he recovered, he told Mihalis, "I want to go back to the camp. Because I'm not afraid. What are those guys going to think about my God if I just run away? Even if something bad happens to me, I know that I have made the right decision. So, when am I getting baptized?"

Reflection

Think of all the baptisms you have witnessed firsthand. What did it cost the participants? Pray for your brothers and sisters all over the world whose lives are now under threat because they have taken this decisive step in proclaiming their allegiance to Christ.

DAY 6

THE FIRST FELLOWSHIP

ACTS 2:42–47

They devoted themselves to the apostles' teaching and to fellowship, to the breaking of bread and to prayer. Everyone was filled with awe at the many wonders and signs performed by the apostles. All the believers were together and had everything in common. They sold property and possessions to give to anyone who had need. Every day they continued to meet together in the temple courts. They broke bread in their homes and ate together with glad and sincere hearts, praising God and enjoying the favor of all the people. And the Lord added to their number daily those who were being saved.

WHEN MOVEMENTS start, things are simple and beautiful. In the earliest days of the church, there was no need for elders or deacons yet. No need for structure. No debates that would later impact the church. They were just Jews celebrating the Messiah. For many, this is a portrait of what a church should be.

Acts 2:42–47 is one of the most cherished snapshots of the early church. About three thousand people embraced the gospel message, turned to Christ, and were baptized. They joined the small community of disciples, forming the first church. Look at their activities. First, there's a commitment to learning, and the apostles are dedicated to teaching—a perfect synergy when listeners are hungry to learn, and teachers are passionate to teach. Certainly we all know what this is like when it happens!

Second, they meet in various places: in the temple, by the water, in the marketplace, and especially in homes. Wherever they gather, they learn, pray, and worship together. Their hospitality is remarkable. Many in this crowd were strangers who had traveled to Jerusalem for the festival and then converted—yet they welcomed one another into their homes, united by belief in the risen Jesus.

Third, they meet each other's needs freely and without pressure. They're not selling absolutely everything—they still have homes, and the church later includes both rich and poor. But they do share generously, treating fellow believers like family. Over time, this becomes more organized (e.g., certain people caring for widows). The message is clear: These believers are your family, and what you have is for their benefit as well.

It is worth noting that the hospitality must have been extended to strangers. People had traveled long distances to celebrate Pentecost, and it's the believers in Jerusalem who are hosting people. They had been united by the Holy Spirit because of their common belief in the risen Lord Jesus Christ. And it seems that people were drawn to this new movement. People were being saved daily. They were being invited into homes. They were hearing the apostles teach. They could hear the prayers of these believers in the risen Messiah.

How might your church recapture the beauty found in this passage?

Hospitality and the Entry Way to Faith

In a damp green room, there were ten tables where families gathered for tea and a meal. Some would receive food to cook for the week. Upstairs, children were coloring and playing Jenga. At every table, someone fluent in the refugees' language was there, sharing their life and the gospel. Many who came had endured severe trials, and some found faith in Christ in this place. Around 250 people were expected to come through that day. For many, this would be their first encounter with Christians. And the biggest draw? The food.

My friend who ran the ministry that was feeding these refugees shared a story about his time on an island welcoming refugees from boats. One man, soaking wet, arrived with his wife and children. In shock, the man confessed, "There were rumors that Europeans would rape our wives for fun." At that moment, my friend understood the depth of their desperation in a way he hadn't before.

The first step in showing love was a simple meal. This led to prayer and discussions about the apostle's teaching, eventually adding many of these refugees to the number of the redeemed.

Reflection

How might you devote yourself to the teachings of Scripture and fellowship with others through meals and hospitality? Get specific.

DAY 7

THE PRAYING CHURCH

ACTS 2:42

They devoted themselves to the apostles' teaching and to fellowship, to the breaking of bread and to prayer.

THERE ISN'T a lot of private, personal prayer in Acts. Instead, we find the Christians gathering together to pray. Some of you might be the kind of Christian who wants to pray quickly to get to whatever you need to do. My friend calls quick prayers "hungry prayers," as when people pray quickly before meals to then eat.

As you read this passage—a text about the intentional practices of the early church—you may be struck by the thought that you need to learn to pray more. The early believers certainly modeled devotion to prayer, among other practices. But maybe another thought needs to take center stage—the Christians in Acts aren't often depicted praying alone. They pray together. Their praises and petitions are corporate. This is part of the big picture of the whole life they are living in community with one another.

Americans are often hyper-focused on individual spiritual disciplines. We usually pray alone (as Jesus tells us to in Matthew 6:5–6), read the Bible alone, and learn alone. We are drawn to disciplines that we do by ourselves.

Do you know one of the clear signs that the Spirit is at work in a community? It's when God's people pray together. There is a level of vulnerability involved in bringing our joys, laments, and petitions aloud to the Lord together. You might know what it is like to pray with people you don't really know versus people you know well. In this scene in Acts, new believers are still getting to know each other, and yet they willingly jump in. There is a sweet relational dynamic at work—both a growing corporate closeness to God and an increasing interpersonal softness among the people toward one another.

What would it look like for your own community of believers to begin regularly praying together? What would change about your relationship with God? With one another? Can you commit to praying with someone this week?

Praying with Eritreans

I've been at prayer meetings around the world—prayers that go on for hours. Many non-Western cultures have a completely different concept of time and are less hurried in their gatherings. One time I was praying with a group of Eritreans. A woman admonished us from Ephesians 5 to "wake up." That was helpful since it was late at night, and everyone had worked all day. We spent an hour singing and praying, followed by personal confession on our knees. Then we prayed for the church and for each other to be awake—to be attuned to the Spirit of God at work around us and not be lulled into complacency or distraction. We moved on to prayers for protection, for the salvation of people we knew and loved, for those in the community who were actively opposing the church, and for those who were a bad witness for Christ. We continued with prayers for those who had fallen away, for the sick, for the country they lived in and its leaders, and for each other. As the night continued, we prayed for the preacher on Sunday, the choir, the weekly Bible study and movie night, and against evil spirits. All of this was followed by another round of singing, then by grabbing the hand of one person and praying for them, and finally by all of us forming a circle for a closing prayer.

We wrapped up after more than four hours. Everyone had to go home to get to work early the next morning. I remember walking away completely overwhelmed by what I had just experienced. It was a taste of a praying church.

Reflection

How might your church commit to following the example of the Eritrean church and gather to pray corporately?

DAY 8

BE HEALED

ACTS 3:1–10

Then Peter said, "Silver or gold I do not have, but what I do have I give you. In the name of Jesus Christ of Nazareth, walk." (3:6)

IN ACTS, there are seventeen instances of miracles that lead to someone coming to faith—most of them healings. One example is here. Another is in Acts 9. And the language is almost identical. Peter tells both people that Jesus Christ is the one doing the healing and, therefore, to get up and walk.

In Acts 3, Peter and John are in the temple to pray and worship. The man has been carried to a place where he can beg from people who are expressing their devotion to God, hoping for some generosity to be poured out into his life. And so, he asks the apostles for money. Peter probably disappointed him by telling him no. But the disappointment is short-lived, as Peter heals the man. Notice here the man is not seeking Christ, nor has Peter shared the gospel with him prior to the healing. The man wanted money. Peter gave him life.

He is not healed by just any power, but "in the name of Jesus Christ of Nazareth." To say the name of Jesus is to invoke the power of Jesus. This was not a magical formula, but a recognition that the power to heal comes from Christ. The man then jumps up and starts praising God, which led others to be filled with wonder and amazement.

The healing here led to faith in Christ.

Now ask yourself—when Christians have gathered to pray for someone's healing, are they praying for healing alone, or for the name of God to be known through the healing? Stories of healings in Scripture always point to something beyond themselves; they signify the power behind the healing. I have seen people come to Christ because of answered prayers or because God did something profound in their lives, prompting them to respond in faith.

Not everyone experiences healing, and those who are healed eventually die. The Bible doesn't simplify these issues. It doesn't explain why some are healed while others are not, or why some die young while others do not. The mysteries behind suffering often challenge those who struggle with belief. I understand the appeal of the prosperity gospel, which suggests that one can escape suffering through faith alone. However, this is a shallow understanding of the complex and multifaceted ways God works.

Have you ever seen God heal someone?

A Personal Story

On January 12, 2019, I was in pain—as I had been for nearly four years. I suffered from relentless, unexplained headaches, numbness, a broken metabolism, and severe digestive issues that made it nearly impossible to stand for more than twenty minutes. My condition forced me to alter local travel plans, step away from preaching, give up coaching youth sports, and more.

I had sought help from doctors, chiropractors, and nutritionists. I tried countless treatments, but nothing brought relief. My closest friends no longer asked if I felt well; they simply asked how much pain I was in. In the previous twelve months, I had preached only once—and nearly collapsed afterward.

Then, one Saturday evening in Texas, I visited a small group at a church where I was scheduled to preach the next morning. During dinner, I shared my struggles. They gathered around and prayed. Nothing dramatic happened—just simple, heartfelt prayer.

I preached the next day and returned home. A week later, I realized something remarkable: I was pain-free. I hadn't missed a single meeting, hadn't needed to pull over while driving, and hadn't needed a nap. I hadn't changed my diet, workout, or supplements, nor had my stress level decreased. God had healed me—quietly, without fanfare.

My healing is a reminder of God's perfect timing and his kindness to me.

Reflection

Have you ever experienced or witnessed a moment when God answered a prayer for healing, or conversely, when healing did not come as expected? How did these experiences shape your understanding of God's power, his timing, and his will?

DAY 9

BOLDNESS

ACTS 4:13, 29–30

When they saw the courage of Peter and John
and realized that they were unschooled, ordinary men,
they were astonished and they took note that
these men had been with Jesus.

"Now, Lord, consider their threats and enable your servants
to speak your word with great boldness. Stretch out your
hand to heal and perform signs and wonders through the
name of your holy servant Jesus."

CHRISTIANS CAN face various kinds of pushback for declaring Jesus is Lord. The first instance of persecution is at the hands of the religious leaders because of what Peter and John were teaching—namely, that Jesus had risen from the dead. The Sanhedrin (the judicial assembly of elders and religious rulers) had just delivered Jesus of Nazareth to be killed because of the threat he posed to their power and position. Suddenly, his disciples only increased their vocal support of their teacher, claiming that his death had been undone. The efforts to silence Jesus and quash his movement were backfiring on them in the extreme.

In a twist of the ironic, look at what soon follows the arrest of Peter and John: "So the number of men who believed grew to about five thousand" (v. 4). Whoops! That didn't work. The religious rulers could arrest Jesus's followers, but they could not arrest the work of the Holy Spirit.

Imagine being Peter and John, called before the Jewish leadership in Jerusalem to bear witness to their teachings. Just two months earlier, Jesus had faced a mock trial before this same group. Now, Peter and John faced uncertainty about their fate. Could they be crucified too? They didn't know.

Yet Peter, filled with the Holy Spirit, stood up and spoke. Surely the words of Jesus from Luke 21:12–15 were ringing in his heart:

> "Before all this, they will seize you and persecute you. They will hand you over to synagogues and put you in prison, and you will be brought before kings and governors, and all on account of my name. And so you will bear testimony to me. But make up your mind not to worry beforehand how you will defend yourselves. For I will give you words and wisdom that none of your adversaries will be able to resist or contradict."

Jesus promised the disciples that they would not need to rehearse their defense when called on the carpet; the Spirit would provide the words. This promise emboldened Peter and John, even as they stood before the same group who had condemned Jesus. Their proclamation that Jesus is the cornerstone, and their declaration that "there is no other name under heaven given to mankind by which we must be saved," was nothing short of astounding (Acts 4:12).

After they were beaten and released, the church gathered to pray, "Enable your servants to speak your word with great boldness" (4:29). Boldness is not the absence of fear, but the courage to speak despite fear. They understood that true boldness comes from God and that they could not muster it on their own.

This request is not just for the apostles but for all believers. It raises a challenging question: How do we feel about others praying for our boldness? It's easy to pray for others to be bold, but it's a different matter when that prayer involves us. The focus is not on safety, job security, or success, but for the courage to speak God's Word. How can this challenge your response when you are confronted with hardship or opposition because of your faith?

Beaten for Going to Church

Eritrea is the second or third most repressive country in the entire world. My friend Ghirmay recalls living in Eritrea and witnessing a neighbor being beaten for going to church. He once told me, "One Sunday, I heard her being beaten badly, but the next Sunday she went back to church. I decided she must have something real, so I went to church without anyone asking or telling anyone. When I arrived, I felt the love of God for me and became a Christian."

I once met a twenty-four-year-old man who had been beaten multiple times for being a Christian. This persecution didn't stop him from hiking for hours into the jungle to minister to eight families who had become believers, nor did it hinder him from traveling fifteen hours to receive more leadership training.

In Asia, I taught at a church where many up-and-coming church planters bore scars on their backs from being beaten by their Hindu parents for becoming Christians. A year after my visit, a homemade bomb was thrown into the church compound. The church carried on, as this type of persecution had become normal.

Reflection

Take some time to pray for the persecuted church. Pray for those in prison. Pray for those who are worshipping under threat. Pray for gospel workers to go out into these hard places. And pray that you might be bold in your witness wherever God has you today.

DAY 10

THERE IS A MIRACLE RIGHT IN FRONT OF YOU

ACTS 4:14

But since they could see the man who had been healed standing there with them, there was nothing they could say.

HOW MIGHT you react to seeing someone healed right in front of your eyes? You are probably thinking, *Well, of course I would believe.* But this incident highlights a profound truth: Miraculous healings or answered prayers do not always lead people to faith in Jesus. While such events can bring many to faith, others can witness the same event and remain unmoved. The miracle itself doesn't necessarily compel belief; it often reveals a person's heart disposition toward God.

Peter and John displayed remarkable courage in the face of opposition. The religious leaders, taken aback, were left speechless by the boldness of these untrained men. They recognize that these were not formally educated leaders, yet they spoke with conviction and authority. The sight of the healed man standing before them left them unable to refute the undeniable evidence of the miracle.

The leaders' reaction is documented in Acts 4:16–17:

> "Everyone living in Jerusalem knows they have performed a notable sign, and we cannot deny it. But to stop this thing from spreading any further among the people, we

> must warn them to speak no longer to anyone in this name."

The irrationality of their response is striking. Despite witnessing a miraculous event, their immediate reaction is to suppress it, to prevent its spread. They issue threats, commanding Peter and John to cease speaking in the name of Jesus. Nevertheless, the apostles remain steadfast, undeterred by the threats.

What were these religious leaders afraid of? They cannot deny the sign. So, what is it? It must be that they are afraid of being wrong about Jesus—and what it would mean for their influence in people's lives. We are all self-serving by nature and protective of the life we have built. It is hard to have our minds changed, even when something is plainly true. We all have what people call *confirmation bias*. We only see what we want to see. And these leaders, instead of seeing the miracle as confirmation of the claims of Christ, see it as a threat to their own belief and respond by trying to shut it down.

The human heart's response to God can vary greatly, even in the face of clear evidence of God's intervention.

Get Out of Bed and Walk

How often have you heard or even said yourself something to this effect: "If I witnessed a miracle, I would believe."

I have a close acquaintance, whom I'll refer to as Dorothy, who experienced a miraculous healing after being bedridden for a year due to a severe illness. She was sent home by the hospital, essentially to await her death. The hospital even sent her death certificate. However, two charismatic women visited her, prayed, and one day declared, "Dorothy, get out of bed and walk." Miraculously, she did, and she went on to live into her nineties.

Two of Dorothy's sons witnessed this miracle. One, deeply impacted by the event, had his life trajectory changed and became a pastor. The other son, however, does not remember being present and remains an unbeliever.

Even in the face of undeniable miracles, people can choose to suppress the truth.

Reflection

You might know someone who has been resistant to Christ despite his clear work around them. Take some time to pray for someone in your life who has yet to believe the gospel despite God's miraculous appeal to their heart.

DAY 11

AND THE ROOM WAS SHAKEN

ACTS 4:31

After they prayed, the place where they were meeting was shaken. And they were all filled with the Holy Spirit and spoke the word of God boldly.

WHEN THE early church prayed, heaven moved. Their gatherings weren't marked by strategic plans, but by a deep desperation for God. In Acts 4, we find a group of believers turning to prayer not as a last resort but as their first instinct in the face of opposition. And God responded—not just with comfort but with power.

We often admire such moments from afar, wondering whether such experiences are reserved for the early church or the rare revival. But what if the difference is not God's willingness to act but our unwillingness to ask?

Eugene Peterson observed, "Our habit is to talk about God, not to Him."[2] And even when we meet to pray, we often spend more time sharing prayer requests than actually praying. We strategize, analyze, and even study prayer without actually praying. But in Acts 4, we see that God meets his people in prayer—not theoretically but experientially. His presence becomes undeniable. His Spirit fills afresh. His people speak with boldness.

God answers this prayer in Acts 4 in three distinct and remarkable ways. First, he manifests his presence so profoundly that the entire building shakes. This vivid display recalls Moses's encounter with God on Mount Sinai in Exodus 19, where the mountain trembled violently. When God shows up in power, his presence often leads to a tangible, awe-inspiring experience—an unmistakable reminder of his sovereignty and might.

Second, the believers are filled with the Holy Spirit. This filling is not merely a onetime event; rather, it highlights the ongoing need to pray for God's power at various moments. We continually need fresh empowerment, reminding us that spiritual life is sustained by seeking the Spirit's renewing presence.

Last, the result is a surge of boldness among the believers. Assured of God's presence, they speak his Word courageously and remain unbothered by opposition.

The apostle James admonishes believers, "You do not have because you do not ask God" (James 4:2). This call reminds us of the blessings we might forfeit when prayer is neglected. It encourages us to prioritize time with God in prayer with others, seeking his presence and power.

The Welsh Revival

The Welsh Revival of 1904–1905 is an inspiring historical example of the power of such prayer. Led by a twenty-six-year-old man named Evan Roberts, who had little formal training, this revival saw roughly 150,000 people in Wales come to faith in Christ. Roberts's motto, "Bend the church to save the world," captured the essence of their mission. In 1905 he had begun to pray for the Holy Spirit to fill him. Roberts wrote:

> I felt a living power pervading my bosom. It took my breath away and my legs trembled exceedingly. This living power became stronger and stronger as each one prayed, until I felt it would tear me apart. My whole bosom was a turmoil and if I had not prayed it would have burst . . .

> I fell on my knees with my arms over the seat in front of me. My face was bathed in perspiration, and the tears flowed in streams. I cried out, "Bend me, bend me!!" It was God's commending love which bent me . . . what a wave of peace flooded my bosom. . . . I was filled with compassion for those who must bend at the judgement, and I wept. Following that, the salvation of the human soul was solemnly impressed on me. I felt ablaze with the desire to go through the length and breadth of Wales to tell of the savior.[3]

The revival had profound societal impacts, transforming the lives of even the toughest individuals, such as coal miners. The miners' conversion was so radical that the "pit ponies" in the mines, accustomed to their handlers' foul language and rough demeanor, had to be retrained to respond to kinder commands. The revival led to a significant reduction in crime, leaving courts and jails largely empty and policemen with little to do.

Such historical accounts remind us of the incredible potential of earnest, faith-filled prayer. They challenge us to seek God wholeheartedly, ask boldly for his presence and empowerment, and speak fearlessly about the transformative power of Jesus Christ in our lives and the world.

Reflection

Gather some people in church and start praying for God to "bend the church to save the world." Pray for the Lord to break down the barriers keeping people around the world from turning to Jesus.

DAY 12

A FALSE REPUTATION BUILT ON THE BACKS OF THE POOR

ACTS 5:1–11

Now a man named Ananias, together with his wife Sapphira, also sold a piece of property. With his wife's full knowledge he kept back part of the money for himself, but brought the rest and put it at the apostles' feet. (5:1–2)

ANANIAS, WHOSE name means "God is gracious," and Sapphira, whose name means "beautiful," are the first two Christian hypocrites in the early church. Up to this point, the early church has no documented internal conflict, and no false teachers have appeared. Everything seems to be going well. Yet the first sin reported is that of two people trying to enhance their reputations at the expense of the poor.

Joseph had recently sold land and laid the total proceeds at the apostles' feet. In recognition, he was called Barnabas, meaning "Son of Encouragement." Ananias and Sapphira observe this and follow suit, bringing money to the apostles—but quietly reserving part for themselves. Appearing to give it all, they were under no obligation to donate the entire sum. Peter's words in verse 4 cut to the heart of the matter:

> "Didn't it belong to you before it was sold? And after it was sold, wasn't the money at your disposal?"

The issue is not the amount, but their deceit. They wanted the prestige of total sacrifice without enduring the cost.

By keeping some of the proceeds, Ananias essentially committed embezzlement in the name of generosity. He might have promised the entire sale price in advance yet reneged while retaining the image of a fully devoted giver. As one commentator notes, "They [Ananias and Sapphira] wanted the prestige of sacrificial generosity without the inconvenience."[4] Their tactic exploited the genuine needs of fellow believers to elevate themselves—mirroring the sin at Babel, where people strove to "make a name" at the expense of obedience (Genesis 11:4). This offense was neither impulsive nor accidental; Ananias and Sapphira planned it together.

Does that happen now? Consider times when mission projects end up burnishing the reputation of the wealthy while sidelining the poor. Have you been tempted to make a name for yourself at the expense of the poor?

Vacations with a Purpose?

The motivations to serve others are notoriously hard to untangle. A sincere wish to help often mingles with the desire for others to see us as helpful. Sometimes affluent families send their children to work among the poor primarily to teach them gratitude. The mission can become about our image more than about the people in need.

All too frequently, generosity is tied to enticing travel and personal fulfillment. The farther from home we go, the more "spiritual" it seems. The more exotic or "dangerous" the destination, the more impressive the story. Some groups even market these endeavors as "vacation with a purpose," raising the question: Are we doing it for the needy or for ourselves?

One church bulletin exemplifies this mindset:

> We'll spend the week of June 11–18 in Guadalajara (also known as the shopping capital of Mexico), where we will have the incredible opportunity to minister to, pray for, and teach women in a vibrant church community. And this trip isn't a "rough-roach-in-your-bed" kind of experience either. We'll be housed in nice, clean hotel rooms, eat lots of salsa, and have plenty of time to shop! Our hope is to take at least fifteen women (including teenager daughters) on this Mexican Ministry Outreach . . . We trust that God will expand our hearts for Him as He expands our ministry to the women of Guadalajara. If you're remotely interested in this adventure—or if you're just in the mood for Mexico after all this winter weather—call for more details about this fantastic outreach opportunity.[5]

What is happening here? We are using the poor to make a name for ourselves and marketing the mission of God as vacation. We are normalizing generosity without sacrifice.

Reflection

Consider ways your church or ministries you know are using the poor to build up their reputation. What do the poor really need? In what ways can we reflect the heart of Christ in our responsible approach to ministry in needy places?

DAY 13

WHEN GOD IS NEAR, THINGS ARE DIFFERENT

ACTS 5:1–11

"Ananias, how is it that Satan has so filled your heart that you have lied to the Holy Spirit?" (5:3)

Peter said to her, "How could you conspire to test the Spirit of the Lord?" (5:9)

LET'S TAKE another look at the story of Ananias and Sapphira. This is the first recorded time that early Christians test God, and God acts immediately. When sin challenges evidence of his presence, God's response is often severe because a lack of response could be taken as a sign of absence.

The word *testing* carries significant theological meaning. In Exodus, God tests the Israelites multiple times to see how they will respond. Will they trust him or not? Their mistrust reverses the testing; instead of God testing them, the people end up testing God. In Deuteronomy 6:16, we read, "Do not put the LORD your God to the test as you did at Massah." This theme is echoed in Psalm 78:18, 41:

> They willfully put God to the test by demanding the food they craved. . . . Again and again they put God to the test; they vexed the Holy One of Israel.

Consider 1 Corinthians 11:17–32, a passage many churches read during communion. Verses 29–30 offer a strong warning:

> For those who eat and drink without discerning the body of Christ eat and drink judgment on themselves. That is why many among you are weak and sick, and a number of you have fallen asleep.

Since God is present, there should be reverence and purposefulness when celebrating the gracious act of God in sending Jesus to die and be raised. To take the bread and cup casually, in an unworthy way, is to invite judgment.

This is similar to the letter to Thyatira in Revelation 2:18–29. Jesus says that since the church has not been able to deal with the false teacher, his direct intervention is necessary. He will cast her on a sickbed. Becoming sick is a common manifestation of judgment in the Bible. She will be seriously ill—possibly to bring her to repentance. With Ananias and Sapphira, God shows he is not deceived. In Thyatira, he does not tolerate his people being deceived.

God does not impose this type of immediate physical discipline every time. If he did, there would be no one left in the church. But sometimes he does it to remind us that he is God (Acts 5:11). It seems that the more obviously God reveals himself, the more dangerous it is for people who encounter him. Consider how gracious God has been by not intervening in your life in such a drastic way. Reflect on the ways you might need him to.

Intervention in Australia

Don Carson once shared a story about a young pastor who had just completed his seminary education and was sent to lead a church in a small town in Australia. The only church in the town was his Baptist church, and many people attended simply because it was the community church. Upon arrival, he discovered that many attendees were not genuinely converted, and some members were involved in an embezzlement scheme in the community.

He couldn't employ any type of church discipline because the church leaders were involved as well. So he did what he thought was best—he just preached faithfully, but to his dismay, it was received as a polite message and brought little change. Determined to influence a different response, he doubled down, but as a young man in his twenties, the pastor grew increasingly disheartened by the lack of progress despite his preaching, praying, and evangelizing efforts over the course of two to three years.

Frustrated and feeling overwhelmed, the pastor dedicated three months to fervent prayer, prostrating himself before God with tearful pleas. He asked the Lord to either send a stronger person to handle the difficult situation or to intervene directly and rectify the problems plaguing the church. After three months of tearful prayers, the young pastor began to perform funerals, thirty-four in total, many of which were for the church's leaders. In the following year, he baptized two hundred people.

Reflection

How might you take God more seriously?

DAY 14

SIGNS AND WONDERS

ACTS 5:12

The apostles performed many signs and wonders among the people. And all the believers used to meet together in Solomon's Colonnade.

I SPEND a lot of time talking about "signs and wonders" in this devotional. Let me give you a big picture overview and some cautions as you evaluate signs and wonders in Acts and today.

First, signs and wonders can occur in other religions. For instance, in Exodus 7–8, Egyptian magicians replicate some of Moses's miracles, suggesting that these magicians have access to real power. Similarly, 2 Thessalonians 2:9–10 describes a servant of Satan performing signs and wonders, and Revelation 13 mentions the second beast performing great signs. These passages highlight that supernatural acts occur in various religious contexts and are not all from God.

Second, false prophets within the believing community may also perform signs. Deuteronomy 13:1–5 warns against prophets who lead people to follow other gods, even if their signs come true. While signs and wonders can be real, the accompanying message may still be false. Jesus also warns in Matthew 7:21–23 about those who perform miracles in his name but do not truly follow him.

Third, Jesus condemns the seeking of signs as proof of faith. In Matthew 12:38–39, Jesus rebukes a generation asking for signs, declaring that only the sign of Jonah (symbolizing his resurrection) would be given. This criticism targets those who reduce Jesus's miraculous works to mere spectacles. The desire for continual signs can stem from a skeptical or consumerist mindset, expecting God to perform on demand. I have a fourteen-year-old named Eli in my life. Eli is awesome. He calls me "little boss," and I call him "big boss," even though I have been his dad's boss and close friend. Every time I walk into his house, he says, "Show me the trick. Show me the trick." It's lighthearted because he knows it's just a card trick. But this attitude mirrors the people who say, "Hey, show me something."

Fourth, believers should find sufficient evidence of God's plan of salvation in Scripture. The Gospel of John emphasizes that the recorded signs are enough for belief (John 20:30–31). Modern-day stories of miracles should not overshadow the foundational truths presented in the Bible. The greatest sign, the resurrection of Jesus, remains the central proof of God's power and love. This serves as a reminder to keep our focus on the core message of the gospel rather than be distracted by contemporary miraculous claims.

There's a tendency to repeatedly say, "Show me another, show me another," essentially asking for miracles on demand. This is saying, "Well, that's not enough." If you find yourself there, asking for more signs, you need to hear Jesus's words of warning. You are essentially asking God to make you the center of the universe, the arbiter of what he can and cannot do. It's as if God must earn your belief by performing one more trick. Jesus says in Matthew 12:39–40 that the only sign you'll get is the sign of Jonah, which refers to his death and resurrection. This is the greatest sign possible: the Son of God crucified for you and resurrected three days later. That is mercy.

When I share stories, I sometimes wonder if I should. They are often illustrations of scriptural passages, but it seems that many people remember the stories and forget the Bible. It should be the other way around.

Tell Me Another Story

As we continue studying Acts, I want to emphasize that what Scripture has recorded is enough for belief. The Gospel of John makes this clear at its conclusion.

> Jesus performed many other signs in the presence of his disciples, which are not recorded in this book. But these are written that you may believe that Jesus is the Messiah, the Son of God, and that by believing you may have life in his name. (20:30–31)

Even if no new stories of miracles were shared, what God has given us in his book is sufficient. The real question is whether you will remember the stories I've shared, or Jesus himself. If you find yourself more amazed by contemporary stories than the signs and wonders recorded in Scripture, your priorities are out of balance.

Reflection

What is the draw of modern miraculous stories? Are you more drawn to miraculous stories than the words God has given us in Scripture?

DAY 15

A CHURCH CONFLICT AND RECONCILIATION

ACTS 6:1–4

In those days when the number of disciples was increasing, the Hellenistic Jews among them complained against the Hebraic Jews because their widows were being overlooked in the daily distribution of food. (6:1)

THE FIRST church conflict recorded in history was over food.

As the church grew, some people in need were not receiving the food they required. The complexity of the community had outgrown the previous methods of distribution, resulting in growing pains. This church was no longer just a fledgling plant or a movement; it required more foundational support, much like a building needs proper foundations, walls, and electrical work. It needed structure. So, how did the leaders respond to this challenge?

They said, "It would not be right for us to neglect the ministry of the word of God in order to wait on tables" (6:2). The church leaders saw their primary role as shepherding through teaching, rather than being involved in the daily distribution of food. Does this seem callous or un-servant-like? Why were they not willing to take on this work?

These leaders had walked with Jesus and had been taught to wash each other's feet, put others first, serve the least among them, and remember that the first shall be last and the last first. They had heard Jesus warn that not feeding those in need would indicate a lack of genuine faith. Despite all this, they chose to delegate this task, which also involved navigating cultural dynamics.

The Greek Jews (considered outsiders) brought a complaint against the Hebraic Jews, who were the majority. The minority group felt neglected and possibly thought, *Here we go again, not being treated as equals*. In response, something remarkable happened. The Hebraic Jews appointed seven men to oversee the distribution of food, and all seven were Greek Jews. This action demonstrated a complete commitment to inclusivity and ensured that the Greek Jews felt represented. It's like if a few Asian believers in a church made up of mostly Africans pointed out that they were being overlooked, and the church responded by appointing Asian believers to leadership positions to demonstrate inclusion. The primary role of these appointees was not merely administrative but focused on peacemaking and ensuring fair treatment for all members.

Handing Over Leadership

My friend Matt helped plant an Afghan church. As you might guess from his name, Matt isn't Afghan—nor were any of the others who helped launch the church. But from the very beginning, their goal wasn't to hold on to power. It was to serve.

As the church grew, Matt and his team remained focused on one thing: raising up Afghan leaders who could one day take the reins. And they did.

Ahmad and Ali were among those raised up. In time, Matt and his team laid hands on Ahmad and commissioned him as the pastor. Eventually, Ahmad raised up other leaders too. I met them one Wednesday afternoon at their "servants' Bible study"—a weekly gathering for the church's leadership. Every person in the room but me was Afghan.

And Matt? He now served under Ahmad, taking direction from the very leaders he had once trained.

Reflection

Consider how you might appoint leaders in your own communities in ways that ensure inclusivity and fairness for everyone.

DAY 16

GOD'S IRRESISTIBLE PRODDING

ACTS 7–8:1

Then the high priest asked Stephen, "Are these charges true?" To this he replied: "Brothers and fathers, listen to me!" (7:1–2)

And Saul approved of their killing him. (8:1)

STEPHEN HAS been dragged in front of the religious leaders on the trumped-up charges that he speaks against the temple and the law. In answering this charge, Stephen speaks of his loyalty to the law while using God's dealings with Abraham, Joseph, Moses, and Israel to proclaim Jesus as the Messiah.

It's often valuable to ask questions of what's behind the text you are reading. For instance, where did Luke get this sermon? He wasn't present, and neither were the apostles. Who, then, is the source? The answer lies in Acts 8:1: "And Saul approved of their killing him"—Saul, the missionary to the Gentiles and a prolific writer of New Testament letters. This sermon, delivered by Stephen, must have profoundly impacted him. Many of the theological themes Saul later articulated in his writings are present in this sermon.

Was Saul convicted by this sermon? In recounting his conversion experience, Saul says:

> "We all fell to the ground, and I heard a voice saying to me in Aramaic, 'Saul, Saul, why do you persecute me? It is hard for you to kick against the goads.'" (Acts 26:14)

The phrase "kick against the goads" is significant. A goad is a sharp stick used to prod animals to move. The image is one of a stubborn animal resisting the prods of its master. Similarly, God had been prodding Saul, and Saul had been resisting.

What were these goads? Certainly, Stephen was one of them. He not only preached the gospel but also prayed that God would forgive Saul, even as Stephen was being stoned, his face shining like that of an angel.

Saul's escalating threats against the church may have been his way of resisting God's push. Stephen preached the gospel to him, telling him that Jesus was the Messiah. Saul responded by killing Stephen. The more God prodded, the harder Saul pushed back, not realizing that he was being cornered by the divine chess player. Ultimately, God's persistent pursuit led to Saul's conversion, a reminder that God's grace can reach even the most resistant hearts. Checkmate was coming whether Saul saw it or not.

Have you ever, like Saul, kicked against the goads when God was prodding you? What did it take for you to stop resisting?

The Lord Is Still Pursuing People

After a long day of meetings, I drove from Minneapolis to Jamestown, North Dakota. Upon arriving at my hotel, I faced an unexpected hiccup: They couldn't find my reservation. When I showed them my confirmation information, it turned out I had accidentally booked for the following Wednesday. With no rooms available, I quickly searched online for another hotel, picked one from the screen, and drove a few miles down the road.

When I entered this new hotel, I noticed the man at the front desk had an ESV Study Bible. Out of curiosity, I asked him about it. To my surprise, he had bought it to challenge his Christian friends about their faith.

I engaged him in a conversation, asking questions. Coincidentally, I had recently been with some of the individuals responsible for editing that very study Bible. His reaction was a mix of disbelief and intrigue, and he repeatedly asked, "I can't believe you just walked in here. Why is this happening?"

I appreciated his authenticity. He posed thought-provoking questions and shared his confusion about churches he'd visited. Our dialogue veered into deep topics like the resurrection, ancient manuscripts, Old Testament rules, and more. I asked him to give me his best arguments against the resurrection, and then I provided the best argument for it, encouraging him to start there and work backward through his other questions.

This encounter felt like a divine redirect. Why else would I, out of the blue, decide to stay in Jamestown (which I had never done before), mistakenly book a hotel for the wrong dates, and randomly end up at his hotel? And why was he there that night, with the ESV Study Bible out, if not to meet an ambassador of the gospel?

Reflection

We all have people whom we long to see come to Christ. How might you be the answer to someone's prayer—for a Christian like you to step into the life of someone they love? Are you ready to share the gospel unexpectedly—at a hotel, or anywhere the Lord might place you?

DAY 17

MIGRATION AND WITNESS

ACTS 8:4

Those who had been scattered preached the word wherever they went.

MOVING IS hard for anyone. Being forced to move without notice due to factors out of your control is something else entirely. I want you to see through this story how God can transform something intended for harm into an opportunity for good, like in the story of Joseph, who told his brothers, "You intended to harm me, but God intended it for good to accomplish what is now being done, the saving of many lives" (Genesis 50:20). Similarly, God has plans for this displacement of his people—big plans.

The fallout from the death of Stephen and the persecution driven by Saul leads to the scattering of Christians. In the book of Acts, we observe the scattering of Christians as a catalyst for spreading the gospel in several ways:

- Involuntary scattering of Christians: Believers become missionaries in new locations, spreading the gospel message wherever they went.
- Relocation of non-Christians: This movement brings nonbelievers into proximity to the gospel message.
- Diaspora communities: These Jewish communities serve as entry points for the gospel, facilitating its spread across different regions.

Acts 8 provides a clear example of this involuntary scattering of Christians. They are dispersed so that the gospel can be proclaimed more widely. As we remember from Acts 2, non-Christians are brought into proximity to the gospel during a festival in Jerusalem, which leads to people from various regions hearing the gospel. This can be likened to international students who might encounter Christianity for the first time at a church near their university. Then there are the dispersed communities throughout Acts that Paul and Barnabas first came to when entering a city. Those Jewish communities did not just magically appear. People had moved!

This involuntary scattering in Acts 8 ultimately leads to significant missionary work among the Gentiles and eventually to the establishment of a church in Antioch, from which a missions movement is launched. Why does God move people? Consider Paul's words in Acts 17:

> "From one man he made all the nations, that they should inhabit the whole earth; and he marked out their appointed times in history and the boundaries of their lands. God did this so that they would seek him and perhaps reach out for him and find him, though he is not far from any one of us" (17:26–27).

Many of you will live in places where people have relocated from all over the globe. Consider that God may have moved them there for you to share the gospel with them. How might God want you to befriend these new neighbors and share the love of Christ?

The Eritrean Church

An inspiring example of this phenomenon is found in the story of my friend Ghirmay, who is from Eritrea, one of the most repressive countries in the world. You might remember his story (see p. 29).

He witnessed his neighbor being beaten by her family for attending church, yet she courageously continued to go. Ghirmay, like many others, fled Eritrea and found himself in Khartoum, Sudan. There, a tape with a sermon on it led him to become a Christian. His journey continued to Greece, where he helped start an Eritrean church. Over twenty years, this church, which typically had twenty to fifty attendees, helped establish congregations in Germany, London, and Toronto, baptizing nearly one thousand people—an impressive average of fifty baptisms per year.

So, why does God scatter people? The scattering, though often seen as a hardship, is used by God to spread the gospel to places and people that might otherwise never hear it. This scattering is a divine strategy, turning displacement into an opportunity for the gospel to reach further and wider than ever imagined.

Reflection

When life forces us to move in ways we didn't plan, God remains at work behind the scenes, weaving his redemptive purpose into our displacement. How might God be using your current location or circumstances to extend his kingdom?

DAY 18

SAMARIA

ACTS 8:4–5, 14

Those who had been scattered preached the word wherever the went. Philip went down to a city in Samaria and proclaimed the Messiah there. . . . When the apostles in Jerusalem heard that Samaria had accepted the word of God, they sent Peter and John to Samaria.

SAMARIA! IF you had asked any of the early Jewish Christians whether they'd ever imagined finding themselves proclaiming the gospel in this land, they would have laughed in your face. Samaria had a bad reputation, and every self-respecting Jew skirted around it every time they traveled. It was defiled.

To Jewish eyes, Samaritans were ethnic and religious traitors. When Israel had split into Northern and Southern kingdoms centuries earlier, Samaria became the capital of the Northern Kingdom. The Samaritans were the descendants of the people left in the land after the exile. They intermarried with others in the region and believed they were the true people of God, dismissing Jerusalem's importance. They worshipped at a different site, had a different temple, and even had their own version of the Torah. To Jews, Samaritans were neither truly Jewish nor fully Gentile.

Luke 9 illustrates how the kingdom of God turns the status quo upside down. Near the end of Jesus's earthly ministry, he set out resolutely toward Jerusalem. Along the way, he intentionally journeyed through a Samaritan village—a choice that would have offended most Jewish nationalists.

He sent messengers ahead to prepare a place for him to lodge, but they were turned down because "he was heading to Jerusalem" (Luke 9:53). The prejudice and bitterness worked both ways. This rejection prompted James and John to suggest calling down fire from heaven on this village. Jesus, however, smothered their wrath.

Fast forward to Acts 1:8, where Luke records Jesus saying, "But you will receive power when the Holy Spirit comes on you; and you will be my witnesses in Jerusalem, and in all Judea and Samaria, and to the ends of the earth."

Right from the outset, the mission of God involved crossing religious, cultural, and ethnic boundaries. They were to take the message of salvation to the outsiders and the despised, including the Samaritans. However, until Acts 8, this had not happened. It took persecution to propel the message outward. Interestingly, it wasn't even the apostles who initially branched out; it was "those who had been scattered," including Philip (8:4). It took a significant event—the martyrdom of Stephen—to push the church outward.

Why did it take so long for them to heed Christ's command? While part of it was due to God's timing, sometimes a push is necessary when the mission gets stuck. When they didn't go out on their own, God intervened, forcing circumstances to get them back on mission.

Consider your life today. Are there ways Jesus wants to smother your animosity toward a particular group or subset of the population? Is there any bitterness clouding your view of who God wants you to reach out to?

Animosity Smothered

India and Pakistan do not like each other. When one national cricket team loses to the other, death threats sometimes force their athletes into hiding. The deep-seated hostility between these groups is serious and often deadly. Yet despite the cultural enmity between these two groups, I once encountered a miraculous sight—an all-night prayer meeting of Pakistani and Indian Christians. Here they were, united in prayer, seeking the heart of God together.

I saw something similar in Europe among Eritrean and Ethiopian churches. Their countries are not exactly friendly, but in this European city, multiethnic churches gathered regularly to pray, share meals, and host services together. The pastors would even sometimes swap pulpits in a sign of unity.

What an incredible view of the impact of the gospel to a watching world! The transformative work of Jesus has the power to bind people together, transcending deep-seated animosities.

Reflection

We often discover that the greatest obstacles to genuine Christian fellowship lie within our own hearts, shaped by deeply rooted biases. How might God be inviting you to replace resentment with grace in your life today?

DAY 19

THE BAPTISM OF AN OUTSIDER

ACTS 8:36–39

As they traveled along the road, they came to some water and the eunuch said, "Look, here is water. What can stand in the way of my being baptized?" And he gave orders to stop the chariot. Then both Philip and the eunuch went down into the water and Philip baptized him. When they came up out of the water, the Spirit of the Lord suddenly took Philip away, and the eunuch did not see him again, but went on his way rejoicing.

HOW IMPORTANT was baptism in the sharing of the gospel? Consider this: When Philip shares the good news of Jesus with the Ethiopian eunuch, the eunuch's conversion is summed up entirely by his urgent desire to be baptized.

Philip chooses to baptize him and, in so doing, declares the eunuch as his brother in faith, despite their differences. The eunuch may have been rejected at the temple, despite traveling for months to be there, but Philip welcomes him into the body of Christ. Baptism isn't just something you do; it's something you receive. It's our initiation ceremony. It's not optional; it's an obligation commanded by Jesus.

There is a fear and hesitancy around baptism. For those new to faith, baptism can be daunting. It may cost friendships and relationships or even lead to misunderstandings with family members who might think you're joining a cult. Declaring your faith publicly through baptism signifies a serious commitment.

People often delay baptism for various reasons. I was one of those people. The gospel profoundly impacted me in college, yet I watched others get baptized while I refused, thinking I was above it. In retrospect, I misunderstood the depth of my commitment to Jesus.

Have you and your household been baptized? What is holding you back? Are there people who you would be hesitant to baptize? Why?

Baptisms Around the World

Baptism is a powerful declaration of allegiance to Christ, witnessed all over the world. My friend has baptized men in a hotel in Khartoum, where Christians do this by discreetly pouring water on each other indoors, as doing so outside could lead to death. I've been with former Muslims who converted to Christianity and were baptized in the Adriatic Sea, risking their lives to publicly declare their faith in Christ. I have been in India, along streams by the roadside in Hindu villages, where people boldly declare their rejection of a multitude of gods, affirming their belief in the one true God through baptism.

But what is equally amazing is that someone stands in the water with them. Sometimes it's someone who once experienced persecution from the person they are baptizing. Other times the person is baptizing someone they once held prejudice against. Baptism is the act of two people and often speaks of the power of the gospel to transform both hearts—that of the person being baptized, as well as the one baptizing them.

Reflection

In baptism, we don't merely witness one person's decision for Christ; we also see the church reaching out in welcome, declaring, "You belong among us." Where might you need to extend that same gospel embrace?

DAY 20

FROM MURDERER TO MISSIONARY

ACTS 9:1–9

As he neared Damascus on his journey, suddenly a light from heaven flashed around him. He fell to the ground and heard a voice say to him, "Saul, Saul, why do you persecute me?" "Who are you, Lord?" Saul asked. "I am Jesus, whom you are persecuting," he replied. "Now get up and go into the city, and you will be told what you must do." (9:3–6)

ONE OF the most influential events in Christian history, aside from the life, death, and resurrection of Jesus of Nazareth, is the conversion of Saul. This event is so significant that it is recounted twice in the book of Acts, an emphasis given to no other account. Saul, later known as Paul, authored half of the books of the New Testament and was instrumental in spreading the Christian faith throughout the Roman world. His writings have been discussed perhaps more than any other in history.

Saul had certainly heard the Christian message and knew what believers were saying about Jesus, but he did not initially hear it as good news; it was a threat that had to be stamped out—whatever the cost. This elite Pharisee, this fervent persecutor of the church, suddenly has a dramatic encounter with Jesus. He comes face-to-face with the one he is trying to stifle. This is the pivotal moment on which his whole life hinges—the moment when everything changes. The murderous oppressor becomes the missionary. The one who once boasted in his resume comes to view it all as rubbish so that he can gain Christ (Philippians 3:8). This transformation becomes a cornerstone in his defense and testimony, as he shares his faith with rulers and others.

These stories of transformation are ongoing today; they are divine interventions. The Lord is still daily drawing the rebellious to himself. Who is the person who in your mind is beyond God's reach? Imagine how God could use their story and background to blaze a trail for the gospel! Commit to praying for them daily.

It Would Be Easier to Convert and Teach These Dogs

Ola and Minnie Hanson were appointed by the American Baptist Foreign Mission Society in 1890 to minister to the Kachin people of Upper Burma (modern-day Myanmar), sent out from what is now Bethlehem Baptist Church in Minneapolis. In the early days of pioneer missions, the Kachin were described as vengeful, cruel, and treacherous. Even the King of Burma remarked to the missionaries: "So you are here to teach the Kachins? Do you see my dogs over there? I tell you, it would be easier to convert and teach these dogs. You are wasting your life."[6] Whether the king just had animosity toward them, or the Kachin were truly terrible people to get along with, it is certain that, like Saul, they did not seem like likely candidates to respond to the gospel.

Despite the challenges they faced, the Hansons remained determined. In June 1911, Reverend Hanson completed the translation of the New Testament into the Kachin language, and by 1926, he had finished translating the Old Testament. To ensure accuracy, Hanson closely observed how the Kachins used their tongues, teeth, and lips when forming sounds. Given the tonal nature of the Kachin language, distinguishing meaning based on tone presented significant challenges. Over time, he compiled a list of 25,000 words, invented the written form of their language, and later edited and published a Kachin-English dictionary with 11,000 entries. Remarkably, while the Kachins were entirely illiterate in 1890, within one hundred years, they had become fully literate in both Kachin and Burmese, the national language.

The Hansons eventually returned to the United States, passed away, and were buried in Nebraska, uncertain of the impact of their work. Unbeknownst to them, the gospel had taken root, and today 400,000 to 500,000 Kachin Christians exist.

Reflection

God delights in transforming the least likely people and the most hardened hearts, just as he did with Saul and the Kachin people. Who might God be calling you to pray for today, trusting in his power to soften even the toughest hearts?

DAY 21

THE MAN IN WHITE

ACTS 9:3

As he neared Damascus on his journey, suddenly a light from heaven flashed around him.

SAUL'S STORY is indeed a sovereign intervention. Many people, reflecting on their own conversion stories, might use a similar phrase, even if they haven't experienced something as dramatic as this pivotal moment.

Blinding and brilliant light often accompanies God's presence in the Bible. Although it was the middle of the day, the light Saul encounters is overpowering. This is the risen Jesus, displayed in glory that had only previously been seen during the transfiguration (see Luke 9:28–36). The light that radiates from him is so overwhelming that it knocks Saul to the ground.

Saul asks, "Who are you, Lord?" The word *Lord* could also be translated as *Sir*. He doesn't know who this is; he doesn't realize who is confronting him because he never believed it could be Jesus. He doesn't know the One he has been persecuting. But then comes the surprise:

> "I am Jesus, whom you are persecuting," he replied. "Now get up and go into the city, and you will be told what you must do" (9:5–6).

Jesus does not share the gospel with him. He simply identifies himself and points out that Saul is persecuting him. This encounter likely shapes Saul's understanding of union with Christ—that God's people are so united with Jesus that an attack on them is an attack on him. Now Saul learns that Jesus is alive, that the resurrection is real.

Saul, the once proud, zealous Pharisee, is now blind and being led into Damascus by the hand, utterly powerless and humbled. The event completely breaks him. During the three days he is blind and fasting, Saul must be rethinking his entire understanding of God. The text tells us he was praying, but it's fair to assume that due to his extensive knowledge of Scripture, he was also reexamining how Jesus fit in the Bible's storyline, and probably reconsidering Stephen's sermon from Acts 7. He also had to reconsider passages like Isaiah's Suffering Servant (see Isaiah 53), the possibility of resurrection, the significance of Jesus's death on the cross, and the fact that he had been persecuting God's people. Later he would make a statement as a man who was deeply humbled: "But whatever were gains to me I now consider loss for the sake of knowing Christ" (Philippians 3:7). Only those who are brought to the end of themselves and have opened their hearts to Jesus can speak like that.

When did God's irresistible call become irresistible to you? What happened?

Jesus Came Near

Sahar is one of my heroes. She was born into a Muslim family. One day, she was stopped by the religious police, who found a Bible, a fake Christian ID, and a book critical of Islam. She wasn't a Christian yet but had been searching. She was detained but was bailed out by her father. They fled to Athens, where they had no money, leading her to despair.

She tried to commit suicide twice but failed. The day after her second attempt, she boarded a bus, crying, and said to God, "God, I just wanted to know who you are. I wanted to know you, but instead, I've lost everything. What do you want for my life? You're not even letting me kill myself." She opened her eyes and saw a church. She got off the bus, thinking, *You're in a Greek country. You don't speak Greek. You won't be able to communicate. What are you doing?* But she went toward the church anyway. To her surprise, there was a sign outside the doors indicating that the service would be translated into English, which she did speak.

She got involved in the church, and sometime later while sitting at home, she prayed and honestly said, "God, it's hard to make the decision. Jesus, if you are real, help me make the decision. I need your help." She didn't know if she was awake or dreaming, but she saw a man walking into the room. Her immediate reaction was, "Please don't come closer, because I can't breathe. It's just too heavy; I can't. You're holy, and I'm a sinner. Do not come closer to me." The man simply said, "Sahar, I told you, and I'll tell you again: I am the only way, the truth, and the life. No one comes to the Father except through me."

Reflection

Saul's blinding encounter with the risen Christ reminds us that God often shatters our illusions of control to open our eyes to his sovereign grace. Where in your life might God be calling you to relinquish control and receive his transforming grace?

DAY 22

IS HE MY BROTHER?

ACTS 9:10–15

"Lord," Ananias answered, "I have heard many reports about this man and all the harm he has done to your holy people in Jerusalem. And he has come here with authority from the chief priests to arrest all who call on your name." (9:13–14)

HAS THE Lord ever asked you to do something that you didn't know how you were going to do? Something so huge and impossible that you had to wonder if you were indeed hearing him correctly? If yes, then you will understand the bind that a man named Ananias was in.

We have no clear idea how the gospel originally reached Damascus, but there was a disciple there named Ananias. We don't know much about him, but we see his humanity in his conversation with the Lord. We are told he is a disciple, and in Acts 22:12, he is described as a devout follower of the law and is highly respected by the Jews. This man loved God's Word and had a reputation for being godly. He would have been one of Saul's targets. When the Lord calls him to help his would-be killer, Ananias obeys, but with some clear hesitation.

It's understandable that Saul's conversion would be met with some wariness and fear. Ananias questions whether he should go to Saul when the Lord tells him to (9:13–16). He voices these fears to the Lord, essentially saying, "Lord, don't you know who this man is?"

The Lord's response seems to gently remind Ananias, "Yes, Ananias, I know who Saul is." Ananias would have known of Stephen's martyrdom and Saul's reputation. He was aware of why Saul was initially coming to Damascus; word had reached the church. Ananias's initial reaction was likely, "Certainly not Saul, Lord!"

God needed to work not only in Saul's heart but also in the hearts of his people. They were preaching a gospel of grace, but even they struggle to believe that grace could extend to one of their worst enemies. Ananias's questions reflect a common struggle in all of us: identifying people we consider beyond redemption. We all have a mental list of those whom we find hard to believe could be recipients of grace, such as those who have deeply hurt us or our loved ones. We might think, *I'll believe it when I see it.*

This reckoning brings to mind stories like that of Corrie ten Boom, who, after being held in a Nazi concentration camp, later preached the gospel and encountered one of her former guards, who wanted to talk about Jesus. Or the story of Elisabeth Elliot, who, though her husband was murdered by the Auca Indians, returned to lead those very murderers to Christ. These examples challenge us to consider the boundless reach of grace and the transformative power of the gospel.

How might God call you to walk by faith even when it seems incredibly hard to move toward someone? Let the people who seem far from grace flood your mind, and pray.

From Bible-Burner to Believer

During a visit to India, I met an older believer who was once a Brahmin, a member of the highest caste in Hinduism. He recalled hearing the hymns of a nearby Christian church during his childhood. As a young man, he was hostile toward Christians—burning

Bibles to heat water, tearing up gospel tracts, and mistreating believers.

He eventually grew up and secured a high-paying job, making what he described as "huge money." But there came a point when his business partners betrayed him and forced him out of the company, resulting in his sudden financial ruin. After that crushing meeting, he decided he would call upon the Lord he once despised.

Although his financial difficulties didn't disappear, he found peace in his heart. He remembered the songs he had heard as a child, and this led him on a journey to faith in Jesus. His wife also came to faith, but the rest of his family excommunicated him. This man, who once burned Bibles, now owns many and carries one with him eagerly as he proclaims the good news.

How hard do you think it was for the Christian community to welcome the man who burned their Bibles and mistreated them?

Reflection

Ananias's hesitation before approaching Saul mirrors our own doubts about whether certain people could ever be reached by grace. Who is the one person you struggle to believe God could change—and how might you be invited to display his grace to them today?

DAY 23

CONFRONTING THE BROKENNESS OF THE WORLD IN JESUS'S NAME

ACTS 9:36

In Joppa there was a disciple named Tabitha (in Greek her name is Dorcas); she was always doing good and helping the poor.

HAVE YOU ever thought about the way your own faithful obedience to the Lord is impacting the lives of those around you?

After Paul's conversion, the narrative shifts back to Peter and his encounter with a young girl in Joppa named Tabitha. I want you to notice a few things about Tabitha and her impact in her community.

First, through her, God expresses his love to one of the most vulnerable groups of the time: widows. These women have no safety net and likely no adult children to care for them. They only have Tabitha. Helping those without help was a hallmark of the early church. For all eternity, it will be known that Tabitha was always doing good and helping the poor. Upon her untimely death, Peter goes upstairs to the room where Tabitha is lying and the widows are crying and showing him the clothes Tabitha had made for them.

"Look, Peter, look at the way she loved us."

Tabitha, in her small way, confronts the brokenness of this world. She confronts the death that had left these women widowed and a system that could not care for them. She also addresses the darkness of the world by alleviating people's feelings of loneliness and neglect.

Notice that Tabitha does not perform miracles. This is important to note because we often get caught up in the extraordinary while missing the simple and quiet ways God calls us to be his hands and feet. Tabitha essentially has her obituary written in the Bible. Loving service is what she is known for. I was reading some obituaries recently and noticed they often centered on hobbies. I thought, *I want an obituary like Tabitha's.* I want people to say they saw the love of Jesus displayed in my life and that I truly cared for them.

You don't need to be like the apostles, preaching and performing miracles. Like Tabitha, you could just work to relieve people's feelings of loneliness and neglect. Are you meeting needs as the Lord gives you opportunities? Do people know what Jesus is like because they know you? That would be the richest legacy of all.

HIV-Positive Mothers

Decades ago, in a large city in East Africa, a pastor led his church to reach out to single HIV-positive mothers—a group largely neglected by the surrounding community. These women were ending up on the streets with little to no support. One evening, a woman who attended their outreach event heard the gospel and put her faith in Jesus Christ. The pastor and his wife invested in her life—discipling her, funding her education, and helping her receive some Bible training. They demonstrated the personal care of Christ.

Fast forward to today, and this woman now ministers to hundreds of women each week, many of whom face the same challenges she did years ago. With her church, she meets their needs, shares the gospel, and equips them to do the work God has for them. By sharing the gospel and discipling these women through her local church, she is making a profound difference. All of this started when a pastor led his church to reach out to a neglected group. Their work is the embodiment of James 1:27:

> Religion that God our Father accepts as pure and faultless is this: to look after orphans and widows in their distress and to keep oneself from being polluted by the world.

Reflection

Tabitha's quiet acts of compassion remind us that God often uses ordinary service to bring extraordinary healing in a broken world. Whether it's making clothes for widows in the first century or caring for neglected single mothers today, a simple commitment to love can echo through eternity. How might God be nudging you to offer the kind of practical help that can change someone's story forever?

DAY 24

THE PATIENCE OF GOD

ACTS 9:41–43

He took her by the hand and helped her to her feet. Then he called for the believers, especially the widows, and presented her to them alive. This became known all over Joppa, and many people believed in the Lord. Peter stayed in Joppa for some time with a tanner named Simon.

CAN YOU point to ways Jesus patiently undid some of the things you have believed?

There is a fascinating detail at the end of this chapter, after Tabitha is restored to life. We read that Peter stays in the house of Simon the tanner. Why mention this? Why didn't Luke simply say, "he stayed in Joppa"?

Tanners were considered unclean by devout Jews because they work with the hides of dead animals. Peter seems unconcerned by this association. Peter is gradually moving toward ministry to the Gentiles.

Just seven years earlier, Peter was a business owner, mending fishing nets—a Jewish man holding traditional Jewish values. Then Jesus entered his life. Consider this: How long does it take for Jesus to bring Peter fully into alignment with God's mission to the nations? Up until this point Peter has had very little interaction with Gentiles.

Peter's story is like an open book, almost as if he has an online record of past mistakes. Despite witnessing miracles—Jesus walking on water, calming storms, feeding thousands—Peter denies knowing him. Yet, Jesus restores him. In Acts, we see Peter as a bold evangelist, performing miracles. But Jesus had told him the gospel must extend beyond Jerusalem. Four years later, the church is still largely centered in Jerusalem. God, committed to his people and to Peter, pushes them outward.

Again, in Acts 8, Peter is nudged toward the Samaritans—a group separated by deep ethnic divisions. Now, he finds himself in the house of a tanner, considered unclean. Soon, God will add to these experiences a vision to lead him to preach to the Gentiles.

Even after witnessing the Holy Spirit poured out on Gentiles, Peter isn't fully on board with God's inclusive mission. A dispute later arises between Peter and Paul when Peter distances himself from Gentiles. It wasn't until about fifteen years after the resurrection that the apostles fully grasp that the gospel is for all people, not just a specific ethnic group, and that God is redeeming individuals from every nation and language (see Acts 15). Fifteen years is a long time.

How long does it take for us to align ourselves with God's vision? How much patience has he shown us as he's knocked down prejudices, presuppositions, or outright pride that has kept us from fully embracing his call and his heart toward the outsider, the group we don't understand, or the person who hurt us in the past? Likewise, how patient are we with others God is working on, even if we don't see them changing at the pace we might desire? Reflect on how God patiently moves Peter toward a complete understanding of his mission. While we can read these chapters in an afternoon, they span years of growth and transformation.

We all need correction, not just as children, but throughout adulthood. We need to unlearn many things that come naturally to us. We often think we are wise, yet even Christians, after years of following Jesus, sometimes realize how mistaken they've been and feel embarrassed by their misunderstandings. God is patient with us. God is patient with you.

The Stranger Who Belonged

Years ago, my friend Philemon, who is Cameroonian, was teaching a group of Greek and African evangelical pastors in the basement of First Church in Athens, Greece. They were all together, while at the same time Athenians were in an uproar because an African immigrant had recently killed a pregnant Greek woman. Protests had broken out. Greek police were turning a blind eye to Greek crowds who were indiscriminately attacking African immigrants. I was there. I saw it with my own eyes. But in the basement of this church, an African was teaching Greek pastors. And the Greek pastors were putting their hands on the African pastors and praying for them.

One of the pastors later recounted how, eight months earlier, a Muslim migrant had started coming to his church's Bible study every Wednesday night. The Greeks were very cautious to let him be there, and many did not want him there. One night he came and asked to speak. He stood up and said, "I'm here all these months. I hear about Christ. I see your love, and I feel like right now is the time for me to ask your permission to come in your church and to be a Christian. I want to be part of your community."

All the people, many of whom had lived their entire lives being unwelcoming to strangers, started crying. The pastor called it a crisis in their own hearts that God had addressed by bringing in refugees.

God is so patient.

Reflection

Peter's gradual journey toward embracing the Gentiles shows us that God's work of correcting our biases often happens in small steps over many years. How might God be patiently challenging any of our positions or attitudes that remain untouched by the gospel?

DAY 25

PETER'S PERSPECTIVE TURNED UPSIDE DOWN

ACTS 10:34–35

Then Peter began to speak: "I now realize how true it is that God does not show favoritism but accepts from every nation the one who fears him and does what is right."

PETER NEEDED to be convinced that Gentiles could be part of the same family as Jews. While he may not have been entirely opposed to missionary outreach to Gentiles, he struggled with the idea of Jews and Gentiles having equal status in the kingdom of God, a key implication of the gospel.

Gentiles did not adhere to the food and purity laws found in the Torah, which posed a problem for Jews. For example, a religious Jewish text from the time, the Book of Jubilees, expresses their sentiments: "Separate yourself from the gentiles, and do not eat with them, and do not perform deeds like theirs. And do not become associates of theirs. Because their deeds are defiled, and all of their ways are contaminated, and despicable, and abominable" (Jubilees 22:16).

Jews feared impurity and idolatry, and there were various ways they dealt with this in the first century. The Essenes, which was a Jewish sect, bathed after every contact with Gentiles. Some Jews considered all Gentiles unclean. Peter lived under these Jewish purity laws, which were part of the Old Testament that distinguished Israel as God's distinct people.

God decides to change Peter's perspective through a vision, fundamentally altering Peter's understanding of Old Testament law. In the vision, God commands Peter to eat unclean food. He refuses until God insists. As Peter ponders the vision's meaning, there is a knock on the door; it's the servants of Cornelius, a Gentile, inviting him to come. Peter goes, listens to Cornelius, and before sharing the gospel, he makes two confessions:

> Confession 1: "God has shown me that I should not call anyone impure or unclean." (Acts 10:28)
>
> Confession 2: "I now realize that God does not show favoritism." (Acts 10:34)

These confessions signify that God's attitude toward people is not based on external factors. God accepts anyone from anywhere. It might seem surprising to us that Peter needed to be taught this, given that he had heard Jesus declare all foods clean as recorded in Mark's Gospel, had read passages from the Torah and Prophets, and knew Isaiah's prophecies about the nations coming to the Messiah. He also knew the promise to Abraham that his descendant would bless all nations. Yet, it took this vision for Peter to fully understand.

Is there anyone you are struggling to accept as a Christian with equal status in the kingdom?

A Jewish Believer Teaching Iranian Christians

I assigned my friend Bill, a Messianic Jew—Jewish by ethnicity but a believer in Jesus as the Messiah—to teach the Bible to a group of Iranian Christians, all of whom had converted from Islam. At the time, I didn't know Bill was Jewish.

Considering the tensions between Iranians and Jews, it seemed like an unlikely match. If you look at the news, you'll see that there's often deep suspicion, and even hostility, between the two groups.

But then something unexpected happened. When Bill announced that he was Jewish, the room grew silent, and the Iranians began to cry. They embraced him as their brother. In that moment, the wall of hostility was shattered.

For the rest of the week, Bill taught, the Iranians listened, and they shared many meals together, united in Christ. It was a wonderful picture of the transformative power of the gospel.

Reflection

When we truly grasp that God shows no partiality, even centuries of hostility can dissolve in the embrace of brothers and sisters made one in Christ. Who in your life might God be inviting you to welcome wholeheartedly into his family?

DAY 26

WHEN YOUR PERSECUTOR BECOMES YOUR PASTOR AND MISSIONARY

ACTS 11:25–26; 13:2–3

Then Barnabas went to Tarsus to look for Saul, and when he found him, he brought him to Antioch. So for a whole year Barnabas and Saul met with the church and taught great numbers of people. The disciples were called Christians first at Antioch. . . . While they were worshiping the Lord and fasting, the Holy Spirit said, "Set apart for me Barnabas and Saul for the work to which I have called them." So after they had fasted and prayed, they placed their hands on them and sent them off.

THE CHURCH in Antioch grew to the point that the church in Jerusalem sent Barnabas to check it out (Acts 11:21–24). Antioch is the first church where Gentiles are converting in large numbers. This is also the place where followers of Jesus are called Christians for the first time. Barnabas is so overwhelmed with what was happening that he goes to Tarsus and recruits Saul to help. This is an absolute miracle, and to fully grasp the significance of this moment, let us explore the origins of the Antioch church.

In a surprising turn of events, Barnabas enlists the help of the very man responsible for the believers' initial displacement into Antioch; Saul of Tarsus is now teaching alongside Barnabas. Then the Antioch church, founded by those he once persecuted, sends him forth as their missionary. This is a powerful testament to the transformative nature of the gospel.

The believers in Antioch, including those who may have known Stephen and were forced to relocate due to Saul's actions, embrace the gospel's teachings so deeply that they welcome their former persecutor as their teacher and missionary. The gospel has so transformed them that they learn from their former persecutor for a year and then sent him out with their blessing.

Imagine the challenge of learning the Bible from someone who had once caused the death of your friend and forced you to flee your home. This story serves as a reminder that the gospel's power to change lives knows no bounds, even enabling us to forgive those who have caused us immense pain and suffering. Are you open to experiencing the transformative power of the gospel in your life and relationships?

Worshipping with Afghans

One Sunday while in Greece, I had the unique opportunity to attend worship at an Afghan church. With only a few hundred such churches worldwide, this experience was extraordinary. That morning, one hundred Afghans, the missionaries who had introduced them to Christianity, and several Muslim visitors gathered to share in the sense of community and the freedom to explore their faith.

The pastor, a former religious police officer, had converted to Christianity due to the kindness shown by the very Christians he had once persecuted. That day, their guest speaker was a Korean missionary. A few years earlier, the Korean missionary had been among a group held hostage by the Taliban for forty days, during which some of his colleagues lost their lives. Now, he stood preaching in an Afghan church, next to a pastor who, only a few years prior, might have killed him.

The teaching time created a remarkable scene. The Korean brother delivered his sermon in English, which was then translated by my Afghan friend to Dari. This multilingual worship service was a powerful testament to the incredible transformation that had taken place within the congregation.

The gospel's ability to forge the most improbable alliances was on full display.

Reflection

The church in Antioch reminds us that God can redeem even our deepest hurts and most unlikely alliances for his redemptive plan. In what ways has God already redeemed some of the hurts in your life or in the life of someone you know? Pray together with a friend about ways you'd like to see unresolved hurts redeemed for God's glory.

DAY 27

FROM BARNABAS AND SAUL TO PAUL AND BARNABAS

ACTS 11:25–30; 13:42–43

So Barnabas went to Tarsus to look for Saul. (11:25)

When the congregation was dismissed, many of the Jews and devout converts to Judaism followed Paul and Barnabas, who talked with them and urged them to continue in the grace of God. (13:43)

WE HAVE encountered Barnabas multiple times as we've made our way through Acts. In today's passage, we see him as the trusted emissary of the church of Jerusalem. Upon seeing the needs in Antioch, he recruits Saul to help teach all the new believers. This leads to a vital ministry partnership in which Barnabas comes alongside a newer brother in Christ and helps him grow in his pivotal role of reaching the Gentiles. All along the way, we see evidence that Barnabas is not out to make a name for himself but is focused on faithful service to Christ so that the gospel may continue to go forward.

I think Barnabas is the kind of man that is the glue that holds together the early church, playing a crucial role as the book of Acts unfolds. One commentator calls him the man with the biggest heart in the church.[7] We see this in Acts 9 when he advocates for Saul before the Jerusalem leaders:

> When he [Saul] came to Jerusalem, he tried to join the disciples, but they were all afraid of him, not believing

> that he really was a disciple. But Barnabas took him . . . (9:26–27).

Three years have passed since Paul's conversion, and he now wants to come down and meet with the leaders in Jerusalem. But they are afraid. Paul needs someone to bridge the gap and advocate for him. So "Barnabas took him." I don't want to overlook that line. Barnabas is the man who welcomes Saul into the church, advocates for him, and paves the way for his acceptance among the very people Saul had once persecuted.

And for the next few years, Barnabas is listed first whenever Scripture talks about the ministry he and Saul pursued together. He is the more prominent leader. Luke, the author of Acts, shows him honor. But something changes in Luke's writing as Saul (Paul) transitions into a more prominent role. Eventually Barnabas will give way to Saul, and starting in Acts 13:42, Luke refers to them as "Paul and Barnabas."

Undoubtedly, Barnabas embraces this change and likely celebrates Paul's rise in leadership. He understands that God had raised up Paul to take the gospel to the nations. He supports Paul's development as a leader through their ministry in Antioch, across Cyprus, and beyond to Asia Minor. Barnabas knows this ministry is not about him; it is about Jesus.

This prompts us to reflect on our own attitudes: Are we able to rejoice when fellow Christians surpass us in leadership positions? Can we celebrate their achievements, even if our role becomes less significant?

The gospel imparts a unique power that enables us to support and uplift others without feeling threatened by their success. Are you willing to show hospitality and give away your authority or influence like this? As we grow in our faith, may we embody the humility and grace exemplified by Barnabas, and embrace the transformative power of the gospel in our mentoring.

Dieudonné and His Barnabas

Years ago, Dieudonné Tamfu, a native of Cameroon, learned that John Piper would be speaking at an event in his home country. Surprised and excited, he attended the event. After hearing John speak, Dieudonné felt a calling to enter ministry, and he approached one of John's ministry colleagues, Tom Steller.

Tom informed Dieudonné that they would be happy to train him at Bethlehem, but he needed to first cultivate some ministry experience, as he was a brand-new believer. In response, Dieudonné promptly planted a church and became a pastor. Eventually, he relocated to Minneapolis, where he lived in Tom's basement for three years while receiving additional pastoral training. With Tom's recommendation, Dieudonné went on to earn a PhD in Biblical Theology from Southern Seminary.

After completing his studies, Dieudonné returned to Cameroon, where he planted another church, founded a seminary, and established a printing ministry. He is a man gifted like the apostle Paul. Meanwhile, Tom, after four decades in pastoral ministry, resigned from Bethlehem Baptist Church to dedicate himself to missions full-time. He now serves under Dieudonné's leadership in Cameroon.

In a recent letter I received from Tom, he signed, "Dieudonné and Tom."

That's the heart of Barnabas.

Reflection

Barnabas shows us that a gospel-shaped heart can celebrate another person's rising influence without feeling threatened or envious. Where is God calling you to step back so someone else can step forward for the sake of his kingdom?

DAY 28

THE KINGDOM ATTACKED

ACTS 12:1–6

It was about this time that King Herod arrested some who belonged to the church, intending to persecute them. He had James, the brother of John, put to death with the sword. When he saw that this met with approval among the Jews, he proceeded to seize Peter also. This happened during the Festival of Unleavened Bread. (12:1–3)

UNTIL NOW, the book of Acts reads like a victory march: The Word of God spreads, grows, and many come to faith in Christ. Saul's conversion and the formation of a multiethnic church in Antioch are significant milestones. Then, seemingly out of nowhere, Herod murders James, marking the second murder (Stephen) of a leader of the Jerusalem church.

This Herod was a savvy political figure who rose to power because of his childhood friendship with emperor Caligula. He maintained Roman peace in Jerusalem by observing Jewish festivals, even offering sacrifices in the temple's court of the Gentiles. A people pleaser, he likely saw the growing Christian sect as a threat that needed silencing. If the religious rulers and the people of Jerusalem became agitated and unsettled, it could affect his grip on power. Consequently, he arrests some believers.

Among those arrested was James, the brother of John and son of Zebedee—one of Jesus's apostles and part of his innermost circle. Herod had James executed by the sword, possibly by beheading him. In Jewish law, beheading was a possible penalty for apostasy, so it is unclear whether Herod viewed James as a heretic or a political liability due to messianic claims about Jesus. Whatever Herod's motive, James's death is a severe blow to the early church.

Seeing how his approval ratings soared after executing James, Herod proceeds to arrest Peter, arguably the most vocal and influential early church leader. To emphasize the severity of Peter's situation, Luke notes that Peter was guarded by four squads of four soldiers each. Two were chained to him and two stood guard outside the cell, intent on preventing any jailbreak. Facing likely execution, Peter's situation mirrors that of Jesus on the night of his arrest.

In Acts 12:1–6, the overall picture looks grim: James has been killed, Peter languishes in prison, and the king in Jerusalem is exercising unbridled power. Herod's popularity has surged, and everything appears to be going his way. What should God's people feel in a moment like this? What comfort and hope can they cling to when it seems like the enemy is dealing a blow to the kingdom of God?

We of course can read the rest of the story and see what God does. But in the midst of it, living through hard times can be challenging when you do not know the final chapter. When things are bleak, where do you turn? What thoughts invade your mind about God and the world that seems at times so out of control?

A Better Way Than Violence

Recently, a friend in Asia sent me a string of messages. I've only fixed the grammar and locations to make it easy to read and keep my friend safe:

> Thursday—A handicapped person who was sitting in front of the house was shot. Today, thirteen people were killed. Last night, they came to our Bible College area and

> tried to occupy our building. We fervently prayed, and they turned in another direction. We did hear gunshots the whole night. A pregnant woman hid young people, but she was shot and killed.
>
> Sunday—We had worship service at 10:30 am at our Bible College Compound Assembly Hall. There were about fifty people. After the worship service, we all departed from the church for our own homes. On the way, we saw a crowd protesting near our house. Soon after we arrived at our house, we heard gunshots and loud noise—people shouting. From our window, we looked outside and saw people running here and there for their lives. Then we saw very thick smoke and came to know that three company buildings were burned near our Bible College building. The owners of the burned buildings are Chinese. In the evening, a hospital worker told us there were 102 dead bodies at the hospital, killed by gunfire. The killing took place near our house. At midnight, martial law was announced. We are now under martial law.
>
> Monday—When we woke up, a news report said that over 200 people were killed on Sunday. In many towns and regions across the country, there were protests, shootings, and killings. Hospitals, schools, and universities are occupied by the army. Civilians are persecuted, tortured, and killed. Pregnant women and children were also tortured and killed.

Rulers today still resort to violence to hold on to their power. It can seem so grim.

Reflection

Faith is tested—not by easy answers, but by deep trust. I think of times in my own life when things felt out of control, when injustice seemed to win, and I had to decide whether I would cling to God's promises or let fear shape my outlook. In dark times, remember that God's kingdom is never ultimately threatened. Even when it looks like evil is winning, God is at work in ways we can't yet see. How might you pray knowing this?

DAY 29

GIVE GLORY TO GOD

ACTS 12:20–13:1

Immediately, because Herod did not give praise to God, an angel of the Lord struck him down, and he was eaten by worms and died. (12:23).

LUKE'S POINT is clear: Opposing Jesus ultimately leads to defeat. The kingdom of God will continue to advance despite humankind's attempts to thwart God's work. Recall that Herod arrests Peter to boost his approval ratings; he is a man who seeks praise. We see him again in verse 21, sitting on his throne, delivering a speech to the people. It is a public event where he wants everyone to see him as the one in control.

Herod wants to be seen as powerful. One writer mentions that his robe was made of silver and shone brightly. The crowd proclaimed, "This is the voice of a god," and Herod, who professes the Jewish faith, fails to give praise to God.

Peter is different. An angel breaks him out of prison, even leading him past the guards that were supposed to watch him. It was miraculous. In Acts 12:17, Peter gathers a group of Christians together and speaks of what the Lord has done:

> Peter motioned with his hand for them to be quiet and described how the Lord had brought him out of prison.

Peter knows it is the Lord who deserves credit for his deliverance. Herod in contrast boasts about his own deeds—he did not give God the glory. The result? An angel strikes Herod down. Luke, the doctor, adds that he was eaten by worms and died. I'll leave it to the medical experts to figure out exactly what happened, but it was certainly not an easy death.

Herod's obituary is essentially the obituary of every person who fails to honor God. He did not give praise to God, which is the fundamental issue for all of us, isn't it? Herod received what we all deserve. Scripture portrays a God who demands worship and a creation that prefers to worship itself—a God worthy of worship and a humanity that loves to be worshipped. Some, like Herod, are blatant about it; others keep this self-worship hidden in their hearts.

But then there is Peter, whose heart has been transformed. He gives all the glory to God for his miraculous prison escape. "God did it," he declares. This is the essence of Christian salvation: God did it, not us. And now the conclusion: "But the word of God continued to spread and flourish" (Acts 12:24).

What a way to end a chapter. God frees Peter from prison. God takes Herod's life. God causes his Word to spread. God will not share his glory with another. He delights in his own praise. How might we live and speak in a way that brings glory to God and not to ourselves?

I Am a Pastor in Africa

We have all been around leaders who lead for the sake of praise. They are driven by their own glory and fiercely protect their reputation. But there are other kinds of leaders. Leaders that are marked by humility. Leaders that are happy to give glory to God.

Ramez Atallah was the youngest presenter at the Lausanne Conference in 1974, where he had the opportunity to meet many prominent Christian leaders of the time. At the 2024 Lausanne

Conference, with tears in his eyes, he shared a moving story about a humble African man who had prayed with him every night. The man had introduced himself simply as "a pastor in Africa." Only later did Ramez discover that this man was Festo Olang, the archbishop of Kenya—an influential leader who played a pivotal role in Bible translation efforts and led the Kenyan church through a period of remarkable growth.

In a letter to his wife recounting the conference, Atallah wrote:

> What impressed me most was the life and actions of these men. I saw great men without the "props" which usually support their greatness, and yet many of them demonstrated that their greatness was more than skin-deep. The joy of the Lord radiated from their faces. They did not try to impress by their knowledge or position. I was encouraged to see the strength of the Church and to know that these men really love the Lord.

Atallah was with leaders who gave glory to God.

Reflection

Herod's pursuit of applause ends in tragedy, while Peter's posture of humble thanks leads him deeper into God's unfolding plan. This contrast reminds us that every gift, achievement, and position we hold is ultimately from the Lord's hand. Where might you need to redirect credit from yourself to the God who truly deserves the praise?

DAY 30

THE LEADERS OF THE FIRST MISSIONARY CHURCH

ACTS 13:1

Now in the church at Antioch there were prophets and teachers: Barnabas, Simeon called Niger, Lucius of Cyrene, Manaen (who had been brought up with Herod the tetrarch) and Saul.

WHEN WE look at the leadership team in Acts 13, we see something striking: it's not just multiethnic; it's multicultural and made up of many social classes and life stories. These aren't just different kinds of people. They are different kinds of leaders—brought together, reshaped by grace, and united for a global mission. The gospel doesn't erase their differences; it redeploys them.

The leadership of the church in Antioch includes a beautiful tapestry of individuals—perhaps the most unlikely of teams. Barnabas, a Jew from Cyprus, is a key figure in the Jerusalem church—an encourager who shows hospitality to those considered risky. He urges believers to welcome newcomers, trusting the full reach of God's grace into their lives. Included in this group is Simeon, a Black African whose name, *Niger*, is Latin for "black." Some speculate that he is the man who carried Jesus's cross. Lucius of Cyrene is a Roman from Libya, another North African region. Manaen, possibly the half brother of Herod Antipas, grew up alongside him and yet becomes a church leader—he may have been Luke's source for some stories about Herod. Last, there is Saul, who had already ministered for fourteen years. Saul is his Jewish name, Paul his Greek name that is used later among the Gentiles.

Imagine the stories this group shared. One leader comes from Herod's household—the ruler who killed John the Baptist and conspired against Jesus. Another, Barnabas, is a peacemaker. Saul had persecuted Christians before his dramatic conversion. Two of them are from another continent entirely. The gospel reorients them to become a missionary people, not just a social club.

Some churches claim to value diversity yet have homogenous leadership. But here, the church's leadership mirrored its varied membership. Too often, we assume diversity is a checkbox for church staff or Sunday visibility. But Acts 13 calls us higher. Diversity in leadership is not cosmetic—it is missional. God uses different voices.

Multiethnic churches feel like an impossibility in an age of polarization. Multiethnic leadership seems like an even greater impossibility. If your church is in a diverse location, how might your church body and leadership reflect the community in which you live?

Five Thousand Christians from Two Hundred Countries

In fall 2024, five thousand Christian representatives from more than two hundred nations gathered for the Fourth Lausanne Congress in South Korea. First convened by Billy Graham and John Stott in 1974, the Lausanne movement seeks global collaboration to fulfill the Great Commission.

Words fail to convey the beauty of worship in that setting. "I believe in the communion of saints," gains fresh meaning when you glimpse heaven on earth. Around my table were a Kenyan priest serving in rural England, a Mongolian working for an NGO helping children, a Japanese professor, an Indonesian doctor passionate about evangelism, and a seminary president also on the NAACP board.

We were very different and often disagreed. At times, cultural clashes and theological variances caused misunderstanding. Yet we are the bride of Christ, unified in the gospel, forever part of his family.

Reflection

The leadership in Acts 13 is a striking picture of how the gospel unites people who would never naturally gather—Jews and Gentiles, Africans and Romans, even former enemies. Where do you sense Jesus calling you to embrace and celebrate the diversity within his body—both locally and globally?

DAY 31

SENT

ACTS 13:2–5

While they were worshiping the Lord and fasting, the Holy Spirit said, "Set apart for me Barnabas and Saul for the work to which I have called them." So after they had fasted and prayed, they placed their hands on them and sent them off. The two of them, sent on their way by the Holy Spirit, went down to Seleucia and sailed from there to Cyprus. When they arrived at Salamis, they proclaimed the word of God in the Jewish synagogues. John was with them as their helper.

ANTIOCH IS serious about sending workers for the gospel. The church lays hands on Barnabas and Paul—a commissioning act symbolizing blessing and support. This release from their Antioch duties allows them to embark on a new mission. And so, Barnabas and Paul go, with the blessing of their church.

These travel narratives in Acts are astonishing, but they are easy to gloss over. We only get a brief mention that Paul and his companions travel from Antioch to Seleucia, then sail to Cyprus. But let's pause to consider what that journey entailed. They walk sixteen miles from Antioch to Seleucia, navigate a 130-mile voyage to the island, and then cover one hundred miles on foot from Salamis to Paphos, crossing two mountain ranges. This was no leisurely trip.

We often gloss over such travel details, but the physical demands were immense. These journeys involve days of hiking through rugged terrain and unpredictable weather, all while securing food and lodging as they went. Acts highlights miracles and conversions, but it omits daily hardships like illness, exhaustion, or bitterly cold nights. We don't even know if they stayed in inns or relied on local believers.

Consider Paul's broader efforts. Historians estimate he walked over ten thousand miles during his ministry—akin to trekking from New York to Los Angeles four times. This was not smooth terrain: mountains, rough paths, and potential threats lurked everywhere. Paul was no mere scholar tucked away safely in a study; he was a tireless traveler who would do anything to spread the gospel.

Imagine the untold stories: sleepless nights in unfamiliar surroundings, soaking rains that made every step harder, or the crushing fatigue from one more mile than he felt capable of walking. Each footstep was an act of obedience, each hardship a reminder that the gospel's advance often comes through perseverance. It was real life, not an idealized mission, demanding grit at every turn.

Reading Acts, we can forget the physical sacrifices behind the scenes. What hardships would you endure—physically or otherwise—to share Christ where He's not yet known?

Risking the River for the Gospel

For nearly six years, Pastor Pedro and his wife Simone have served deep in the Amazon Basin, navigating some of Brazil's most remote rivers. Their mission: to bring God's Word to scattered rainforest communities, often by traveling through perilous waters and dense terrain.

Pastor Pedro regularly visits more than thirty communities along the Curumitá, Tefé, and Japurá rivers. Each trip can last days. In the rainy season, high water eases navigation, but in the dry season, low water forces him to trek miles through thick jungle.

Some villages lie five days away by boat, creating major logistical challenges.

A year ago, his boat capsized on a remote river known for crocodiles, anacondas, and piranhas. Though they survived, it was a close call. Undeterred, they salvaged the boat and continued, compelled by a commitment to reach those who haven't heard the gospel.

Natural threats aren't the only concern. The waters swarm with pirates, and many communities have seen theft and violence. On one trip, villagers believed Pedro was a pirate and prepared to turn him away. He assured them, "I'm a pastor, not a pirate." Over time, trust developed, and now more than one hundred people regularly gather there for God's Word.

Reflection

What sacrifices might God be calling you to make so that his good news can reach where it's least expected?

DAY 32

WHEN YOU HAVE NO BIBLE

ACTS 14:7–20

"In the past, he let all nations go their own way. Yet he has not left himself without testimony: He has shown kindness by giving you rain from heaven and crops in their seasons; he provides you with plenty of food and fills your hearts with joy." (14:16–17)

A FRIEND of mine works with a campus ministry. They were sharing the gospel and the need for Christ at a university campus. And then the student said, "I think I'm understanding what you're getting at. I just have one question: Who is Adam? You keep talking about Adam. Is he one of the campus ministry people I haven't met yet?"

When Paul shares the good news with a Jewish and Gentile audience in a synagogue, he uses large portions of Scripture. This method is like Peter's in the early chapters of Acts, Stephen's before the Jewish leaders, and Philip's with the Ethiopian eunuch. In each case, the one hearing the good news has a strong understanding of the full arc of Scripture. They possess a framework for interpreting God's actions throughout history and how God's work in the world today connects to the story he's been writing for thousands of years. But what happens when people don't have that framework? If you read Acts 14 and 17, you find examples of how Paul connects the gospel to those who don't have a history with God. He engages with the Greeks based on what they know of the world and how their own culture and belief system point to both a higher power and to deeper needs they don't have answers for.

First, consider what people desire deep down. The answer is clear in the text: They desire to connect with a transcendent being. They wanted to label Barnabas and Paul as gods (14:11–12). This reveals a deeper longing—a longing present in every human being. It's why many are fascinated by science fiction and space exploration; there's a desire to discover something beyond ourselves. Every culture has stories—hero tales, folklore, fairy tales, festivals, religious observances—that reveal these deep desires.

Second, look at how Paul addresses their deepest desire. His message meets them where they are, confronting their own worship practices. He speaks of good news, but he doesn't begin with Jesus as the Messiah crucified for the forgiveness of sins. Instead, he starts with turning from worthless idols to the living God.

Paul starts with where the people are. In the same way, we can look for bridges to the gospel in our own culture—points of entry where people are looking for answers. Help them see how the story of their longings—longings for authenticity, power, or the transcendent—are all answered in Jesus.

You can ask people why they feel guilt and how they deal with it. You can ask them why stories where characters give their life for someone are so powerful. You can ask them why they are never satisfied by what they pursue. Or you can have them consider the stars some night and how we all long to reach out to some transcendent power.

Can you share the gospel without quoting the Bible?

Teaching Genesis in Asia

While teaching Genesis 1–2 in the mountains of a predominantly Buddhist country, we found ourselves prepared for all sorts of questions—questions we were used to addressing in a Western context. However, we quickly realized that the questions these pastors were asking were entirely different from what we anticipated. They wanted to know, for example, if the universe was reincarnated from a previous creation.

Our approach to Scripture, shaped by the intellectual battles and cultural challenges of the West, did not resonate with their concerns. It was a humbling moment as we recognized how ill-equipped we were to address the issues unique to their worldview and cultural background. We needed to understand their culture and the questions they faced as they sought to teach the Scriptures in their own context.

This experience deepened our appreciation for the apostle Paul's flexibility when speaking to different audiences. What a helpful call for us to be students of those we reach with the gospel! Let's get to know where they're coming from so that we can more clearly explain the greatest answer they could ever know in the person and work of Jesus.

Reflection

God has woven deep longings for transcendence into every heart, and only Christ's story truly satisfies them. Where might you be called to translate the gospel into the language of someone's deepest desires?

DAY 33

MAKING DISCIPLES

ACTS 14:21–22

They preached the gospel in that city and won a large number of disciples. Then they returned to Lystra, Iconium and Antioch, strengthening the disciples and encouraging them to remain true to the faith.

DURING HIS first missionary journey, Paul makes a decision that many would consider unwise: He chooses to return to the very places where he had been driven out and even stoned. Acts 13 and 14 narrate his journey and the opposition he faces, some of which is very fierce. He had to walk past the very rocks used to stone him and that were stained with his own blood. When Paul and Barnabas return to Derbe, they experience great success, making many disciples with little to no opposition, likely because their opponents had assumed Paul was dead after the stoning. But now, Paul and Barnabas face a significant decision.

What should they do next? If you can visualize a map or look at one in the back of your Bible, you'll see they have the option to head southeast, stopping in Tarsus (Paul's hometown) before returning to Antioch, their starting point. This route would have made sense, especially as there were still unreached people in the region who had never heard of Jesus. Yet, instead of taking the easier, safer route, Paul and Barnabas choose to go back—to return to the very places they had already visited, despite the dangers.

Consider this: the time and energy Paul invests in revisiting and strengthening the believers and their local leaders could have been spent reaching new people who had never heard of Jesus. Why does Paul repeatedly choose to invest his time in these believers? Because Paul understands that Christ's mission is not just about making converts but about making disciples from all nations.

I bring this up because, in missions and local church work, everything often feels urgent. There's always a pressing need or task, and we sometimes lean on this urgency to motivate people to give or act. But Paul, throughout his life, tempered urgency with patience.

After preaching the gospel in Derbe and leading many to Christ, Paul and Barnabas didn't take the quickest route back home. Why? They backtracked to "strengthen and encourage the disciples" and to "appoint elders in every church" (14:22–23).

Paul doesn't leave new Christians to fend for themselves. After people came to faith in Christ, he invests in their growth. Paul has a clear vision for what long-term Christian faith should look like—one that went beyond conversion. He wants to give these new believers a solid foundation to stand on.

Paul sees the missionary task as more than just proclaiming the gospel. His approach was threefold: preach the gospel, instruct believers, and gather them into communities. His work isn't complete until all three steps are fulfilled. Even then, Paul stays connected with these communities, offering further encouragement and support. His decisions reflect his priorities: He is focused on making disciples, not just converts.

Think about the ministry endeavors you are a part of, whether at home or abroad. How might you and your fellow disciple-makers commit to the strengthening and establishing of new believers? Perhaps this will look like a long-term mentorship of a teenager. Maybe it will involve teaching someone how to study the Bible so they can in turn teach someone else. It may not be flashy; it may not catch on quickly. But these seeds will one day grow deep roots for generations to come.

Putting Down Roots in the Netherlands

A few years ago, I spent time with an Iranian pastor who had led a fellow Iranian to Christ and discipled him. The man later moved to the Netherlands, and the pastor lost contact with him. This was normal, as he had discipled many people and simply could not keep up with them. Then, unexpectedly, the man called the pastor from the Netherlands to say that he had led three hundred people to Christ and needed help to teach and disciple these new believers. This man understood that conversions were not enough; they needed to develop deep roots and form churches to sustain their faith. Over time, discipleship multiplies. When we invest deeply in just one person, God can use that life to impact hundreds more. The long-term health of the church depends not just on decisions, but on depth.

And so the Iranian pastor went, not to plant more churches, but to strengthen the believers and firmly plant their faith on stable ground.

Reflection

Even amid urgent needs, Paul prioritizes slow, intentional growth in new believers, appointing leaders and strengthening their faith. Where might God be inviting you to pause and build deeper roots—in your own life or in those you're called to serve?

DAY 34

MISSIONARY REPORTING

ACTS 14:26–28

From Attalia they sailed back to Antioch, where they had been committed to the grace of God for the work they had now completed. On arriving there, they gathered the church together and reported all that God had done through them and how he had opened a door of faith to the Gentiles. And they stayed there a long time with the disciples.

IT'S NOT just those who are sent who should see and rejoice in all that God is doing around the world. The senders are a part of the gospel reaching the nations, and when a close partnership exists between those who send and those who go, all parties can equally rejoice in God's work around the world.

After a year and a half of missionary work, Paul and his companions return to their sending church and provide a detailed report. Luke captures the significance of this moment: They return to the place "where they had been committed to the grace of God" (v. 26).

This phrase, "the grace of God," carries two important meanings. First, it highlights God's protective hand over Paul and his companions—a protection that was evident despite the beatings, imprisonments, and other dangers they face. God's grace had sustained them through every trial.

Second, it refers to the empowerment of their ministry. Paul's ability to preach, teach, and plant churches wasn't due to his own strength, skill, or ingenuity; it was a direct result of God's enabling grace. In essence, this entire mission, from start to finish, is the work of God, not of Paul or his team.

Upon their return, Paul and his companions gather the entire church at Antioch—not just for a brief update, but for a full missionary report. If you've ever attended a missionary report, especially one from people you've supported through prayer or finances, you know how encouraging it can be. These reports remind us that we are part of something much bigger than ourselves. They challenge us to reflect on our own commitments and often help refocus our perspectives beyond our immediate, self-centered concerns.

The focus of Paul's report is crystal clear: They share "all that God had done" (v. 27). Notice the emphasis is not on their own efforts, their strategic planning, or their perseverance. Instead, the glory is directed toward God, who worked through them. This is the essence of Christian mission: recognizing that, ultimately, God deserves the glory. Every success, every conversion, every step forward in the work of the gospel is a direct result of his grace.

How might you encourage a missionary you support to report back to you what God has done so that you can rejoice with them in the work of God? If you are a missionary, how might you frame your updates as opportunities for people to rejoice in the work of God?

Understand the Pressure to Report

Missionary work, like any form of ministry, often comes with a pressure to report results. Those who support and pray for the work want to hear about progress and tangible outcomes. But what should you do when you don't have stories like Paul's?

First, make sure your reports are accurate. There's a ministry I know that has a very active social media presence. Every day, it seems, they're posting about leading someone to Christ in the Muslim world. But the reality on the ground is far more complex.

The truth is that very few of these supposed converts are actually coming to faith in Christ. I once interviewed one of these so-called converts, who laughed and admitted that people were being baptized just for fun, mocking the ministry leaders behind their backs.

Second, you can trust God is doing things you do not yet see. He is often doing more than you realize and your report can be a call to pray to break through whatever you perceive to be holding back your ministry. Even in the book of Acts, there are breakthroughs and setbacks within the same chapters.

When you have stories, encourage the saints. When you are stuck, call them to pray.

Reflection

Paul's report back to his sending church underscores that every success in ministry belongs to the grace of God. When you share about God's work in your life or church, how might you ensure his grace remains at the center of the story you tell?

DAY 35

IN-BETWEEN TIME

ACTS 15:2–4

So Paul and Barnabas were appointed, along with some other believers, to go up to Jerusalem to see the apostles and elders about this question. The church sent them on their way, and as they traveled through Phoenicia and Samaria, they told how the Gentiles had been converted. This news made all the believers very glad. When they came to Jerusalem, they were welcomed by the church and the apostles and elders, to whom they reported everything God had done through them.

HAVE YOU ever had a meeting on your schedule that you knew would be difficult—and, in the time leading up to it, felt nearly paralyzed to do anything else? In doing so, you could miss an opportunity to be used by God as you wait.

The debate over the inclusion of Gentiles in the Christian faith had reached a critical point. It is such a significant issue that it requires a church council in Jerusalem to settle the matter. The basic conflict—whether Gentiles need to adopt Jewish customs to be fully accepted as Christians—is too complex to be resolved in Antioch alone. So, Paul and Barnabas are appointed to go to Jerusalem, where they would meet with other church leaders to discern what God wanted them to do.

But their journey isn't wasted. As they travel, Paul and Barnabas don't merely pass the time. They use the opportunity to share stories of how Gentiles are being converted, and this news makes all the believers very glad. Even in what might seem like an in-between time, Paul and Barnabas take every opportunity to encourage the church.

This trip isn't part of a formal missionary journey. The distance between Antioch and Jerusalem is about 350 miles, and it is probably not a route marked on any map in your Bible as a "missionary journey." Nevertheless, Luke intentionally includes this part of their travel. He could have simply written, "They went up to Jerusalem," but instead, he highlights an important detail. As they travel, Paul and Barnabas share the stories of God's work among the Gentiles, to encourage other believers.. They don't use the time to criticize or stir up division; rather, they focus on lifting up the church by sharing God's grace.

The reaction of the believers is profound—they rejoice at the news. This is their way of saying, "We are fully okay with Gentiles being part of the family of God." And that's no small thing. They are glad—joyful even—at the news of Gentile inclusion.

You never know what might happen during the in-between moments of life. Paul and Barnabas aren't just traveling to help resolve a theological debate; they are building up the church along the way. They use every step of their journey to share in the joy of what God is doing and to encourage other believers.

How can you be more attentive and alert during the in-between times of life? What opportunities might God be giving you to make other believers glad, or to share the work he is doing in unexpected ways?

Ministry in the In-Between

Let me share an example from my own life. Years ago, my friend Eric Terhune was killed while deployed in Afghanistan. I was in Buffalo, New York, when I received the news, and a week later I found myself flying from Minnesota to Kentucky for his funeral.

On my connecting flight, I boarded a small plane. In front of me, there was a broken seat taped off. A woman came on board, and it turned out that broken seat was supposed to be hers. Since the seat next to me was empty, I offered it to her.

We started talking, and as the conversation unfolded, I learned that people had been sharing the gospel with her. I didn't have any agenda or plan; honestly, I wanted to be left alone as I was mourning the loss of my friend. I was on my way to a funeral, but God used that in-between time to work in her life.

Reflection

Sometimes the greatest ministry happens in life's in-between moments. Where might God be calling you to share Christ during those ordinary moments when you'd least expect a divine appointment?

DAY 36

THE FIRST CHURCH COUNCIL

ACTS 15:7–8

After much discussion, Peter got up and addressed them: "Brothers, you know that some time ago God made a choice among you that the Gentiles might hear from my lips the message of the gospel and believe. God, who knows the heart, showed that he accepted them by giving the Holy Spirit to them, just as he did to us.

ACTS 15 records the most important church meeting ever—the Council of Jerusalem—where the heart of the gospel is at stake. The essential question is this: What is required to belong to the family of God? The Jerusalem church rejoices as Gentiles are coming to faith, but the Jewish leadership is unsure whether Gentiles can be fully included unless they are circumcised.

Peter stands up and reminds the assembly of his experience with the Gentiles and their reception of the Holy Spirit. He's actually said this all before to these same leaders in Acts 11, and he reminds everyone that God has already accepted the Gentiles. Peter is at the meeting showing his support for Paul and standing for the gospel of grace.

Peter describes the attempt to impose the law on the Gentiles as testing God (v. 10). In the Old Testament, testing God is linked to unbelief. It's a dangerous practice—remember Ananias and Sapphira? Testing God never ends well. Here, Peter equates testing God with trying to put a yoke on the Gentiles—a burden neither they nor the Jews can bear. If the Jewish believers aren't justified by keeping the law, why would they lay this burden on those who had grown up outside of the Jewish faith?

Peter doesn't argue against the keeping of the moral law (such as the Ten Commandments), but rather the ritual laws that set Jews apart—circumcision, food laws, and other rituals. In the first century, Gentile men who wanted to join the Jewish people had to undergo circumcision and follow all of these ceremonial requirements. Would Jewish followers of Jesus now require this same rite of passage for Gentile Christians?

Peter doesn't tell Jewish Christians to abandon their heritage, and they are free to continue practicing these ceremonial traditions. But those requirements aren't necessary for salvation and weren't to be imposed on the Gentiles. Peter's conclusion is clear: "We believe it is through the grace of our Lord Jesus that we are saved, just as they are" (v. 11).

If we cut through the debate, Peter's bottom line is this: We are saved by grace. The Jews are saved by grace and are free to continue the law. The Gentiles are saved by grace and are free from the law. Rejecting someone based on their adherence to the law is testing God. Salvation is initiated by God through Jesus Christ, and it's all by grace.

The gospel releases burdens. There are no requirements except faith in God's grace through Christ.

The argument of circumcision probably feels very foreign to you. But every culture essentially makes the similar argument—external practices that are required for acceptance. It could be clothing. It could be choices in education. It could be worship styles. It could be anything. We are very good at adding things to the gospel, when in reality they are just burdens that weigh people down. How has God released your burdens? Do you impose any burdens on yourself or others to get right with God? Do these burdens enslave you or free you?

We Are Not Children, but Slaves

It was time for tea. My friend had gone to visit the local Muslim imam. They sat on the floor of the mosque surrounded by a towering stack of books, all inscribed with Arabic writing. Around them were the imam's fellow worshippers—each dressed in long white robes—on the intricately woven carpet. They shared sweets and sipped hot tea, making my friend feel genuinely welcomed.

The imam looked at my friend with a joyful expression, his warm face peeking through his unkempt beard. "Brother," he said, "tonight is a special night for us in Islam. It is the one night of the year when we know for sure that Allah hears our prayers."

My friend gently set down his tea, met the Imam's eyes, and said, "My friend, this is the reality for Christians every single day of the year. We can approach God with confidence, knowing that he hears and responds to our prayers." He paused before continuing, "Like a child approaching his loving Father, we can always be certain that God listens to us." Then, softly, he asked, "Do you have this in Islam?"

The Imam set down his tea, and after a moment of reflection, replied, "No, we do not have this type of prayer. We are not children of God, but slaves. Even my name in Arabic means 'slave.'"

My friend was stunned. The differences were plain to see, and it led to a wonderful conversation about the love of God in Christ.

Reflection

Jesus's invitation to a light and easy burden strips away every self-made requirement, replacing it with the freedom of sonship. Where might you still be living like a slave, rather than enjoying the privilege of a child in the Father's presence?

DAY 37

NAVIGATING DIVISION AMONG BELIEVERS

ACTS 15:39–41

They had such a sharp disagreement that they parted company. Barnabas took Mark and sailed for Cyprus, but Paul chose Silas and left, commended by the believers to the grace of the Lord. He went through Syria and Cilicia, strengthening the churches.

WHAT SHOULD we do when we face significant conflict with another believer? It feels especially disorienting when it happens with someone we respect, love, and have served alongside in ministry. We often wonder: *How can people who each love Jesus and seek to honor him end up in such deep conflict?* That's the question Acts 15 invites us to wrestle with.

We move from the high of the church's unity in Jerusalem to Paul suggesting to Barnabas that they return to the places they had visited on their first missionary journey to check on the believers there. There are no plans to plant new churches; instead, the entire focus is on strengthening the existing believers. Paul's heart is set not only on breaking new ground but also on nurturing the work that has already begun.

Barnabas agrees, but he wants to take his cousin, John Mark, along. This decision sparks significant conflict. This is one of the reasons I appreciate Luke's account of the early church: It's realistic.

Here, we have two towering figures in the faith—men utterly committed to Jesus—yet they find themselves in sharp disagreement.

In the past two chapters, Acts 13 and 14, Barnabas and Paul travel together. They share life, face persecution, and perform signs and wonders together. These aren't just two colleagues; they are friends who deeply trust each other, having served together as leaders at the church in Antioch and as the first church planters in what is now modern-day Turkey. A split between them seems unthinkable. Yet, in verse 39, we read: "They had such a sharp disagreement that they parted company."

How severe is this conflict? So severe that they split up. And after this point, Barnabas is never mentioned again in the book of Acts. Considering the pivotal role Barnabas has played up to this point, the last we hear of him is his separation from Paul. Isn't that astonishing?

The cause of the split is straightforward: Paul views John Mark as unreliable since he had abandoned them earlier (Acts 13:13), while Barnabas is willing to give him a second chance. Paul is adamant—no way. Barnabas, true to his pastoral and encouraging nature, leans toward restoration. John Mark claims he is ready, and Barnabas believes him. Paul, on the other hand, focuses on John Mark's previous failures and questions his reliability and character. What are we to make of this? We are discussing the apostle Paul, who writes extensively about unity, and Barnabas, known as the "son of encouragement."

We should be thankful that Luke presents these two men in all their humanity. Luke doesn't tell us what should have happened. He doesn't tell us to take a side. Instead, we're left to wrestle with the reality that faithful believers, even leaders, can sometimes disagree and go separate ways. But this isn't the end of the story—or at least, it doesn't have to be.

Much of Paul's later writing is aimed at helping believers navigate conflict with humility and grace (e.g., Romans 12:18; Ephesians 4:2–3; Colossians 3:13).

Have you seen splits among Christians? What happened? Why did it happen? Were there missed opportunities for grace, humility, or restoration?

Navigating Conflict on the Mission Field

Imagine how excited you are. After getting a degree that allows you to serve cross-culturally, followed by two years of grueling support raising, then a year of language school, you land on the field excited to get to work. The only problem—your team does not get along. And so now you spend most of your emotional energy trying to play peacemaker with Christian leaders when you just want to share the gospel with people who have never heard the name of Jesus.

This scenario is common. Many missionaries just have a hard time working together. It's not for a lack of love for the Lord. It's just personality and philosophical differences. Just like Paul and Barnabas. Take some time to pray for unity among missionaries. Many work in hard places, and it can be especially difficult if the only other Christian you know is someone with whom you are in conflict!

Reflection

Even the most devoted followers of Christ can find themselves at odds with one another, as Paul and Barnabas did over John Mark. Who in your life might you need to extend a second chance to, trusting that God can work even through deep relational rifts?

DAY 38

DIVIDED, YET DIRECTED

ACTS 15:39–40

Barnabas took Mark and sailed for Cyprus,
but Paul chose Silas and left, commended by the believers
to the grace of the Lord. He went through Syria and Cilicia,
strengthening the churches.

IT IS easy to be discouraged when trusted leaders can no longer work together because of a disagreement. Have you ever been part of a split? What is God going to do with the split of two of the most prominent Christian leaders in the world?

The split between these two spiritual giants, Paul and Barnabas, ultimately results in a positive outcome—the creation of two missionary teams covering twice as much territory. Their disagreement in Acts 15 didn't destroy their love for each other, nor did it prevent a change of heart later on.

Barnabas and Mark revisit the initial stops of the first journey, while Paul and Silas visit the cities from the second half of the first journey. Silas becomes a key figure in Paul's ministry and eventually helps record Paul's letters.

It's worth noting that God does not intervene directly to prevent the split. Although God has spoken through dreams and visions before (as seen shortly after this event, when Paul has a vision), he allows this split between two foundational leaders of the early church to happen. Even after the split, Paul speaks well of Barnabas, mentioning him in his letter to the Corinthians a few years later, showing that the Corinthians were familiar with Barnabas despite the geographical distance of about 1,400 miles between Corinth and the site of the split (1 Corinthians 9:6).

Over time, Mark becomes a close companion of Peter. In 1 Peter 5:13, Peter refers to Mark as his "son," showing a deep, spiritual bond. Mark is traditionally believed to have authored the Gospel of Mark, with Peter as his primary source. Paul also later expresses a renewed appreciation for Mark. In Colossians 4:10, Paul instructs the church to welcome Mark. Despite the initial separation, the relationship between Paul and John Mark is eventually restored. At the end of his life, Paul even asks Timothy to bring Mark to see him (2 Timothy 4:11).

Take heart in knowing that a split, while painful, happened even to the apostle Paul and Barnabas. Yet, over time, they found their way back to each other, and God used it all for the advancement of the gospel.

God Redeems Broken Situations

One of the main reasons my friend Daniel initially went to Brazil as a missionary was because of an ideological disagreement that had caused a significant church split there, directly impacting the campus ministry connected to that local church. The congregation had dwindled to fewer than forty people, most of whom were campus missionaries.

However, this division ultimately sparked growth. Elders began to step up, developing their gifts of leadership and teaching. The church entered a season of deep, committed prayer, fostering a desperate dependence on God and a profound unity of spirit. As God called Daniel and his family of seven to lead a revitalization effort, they witnessed God's miraculous provision as they moved across hemispheres to serve.

By the time Daniel and his family returned to the United States, the church had become healthier than it was before the split, with a flourishing campus ministry and a strengthened church body to support it. God truly brought beauty from the ashes. Perhaps most remarkable was the reconciliation that God brought between some of the leaders who had been involved in the original division. Several who had left the church sought out those they had wronged, asking for forgiveness, which led to Christ-exalting reconciliation.

Reflection

God's redemptive plan is never thwarted by our disagreements. Where might God be inviting you to trust him with a painful division, believing he can bring about unexpected growth for his glory?

DAY 39

REMOVING BARRIERS TO THE GOSPEL

ACTS 16:1–3

Paul came to Derbe and then to Lystra, where a disciple named Timothy lived, whose mother was Jewish and a believer but whose father was a Greek. The believers at Lystra and Iconium spoke well of him. Paul wanted to take him along on the journey, so he circumcised him because of the Jews who lived in that area, for they all knew that his father was a Greek.

HOW FAR would you be willing to go to remove a barrier for others so that they can believe the gospel?

Paul is relentless about one thing: Nothing should get in the way of someone hearing the gospel. The gospel is the free message of grace. He wants everyone to hear it. God had sent his Son to redeem those who would repent and believe. Nothing can be added to that. Acts 15 isn't just about circumcision; it is about whether something needs to be added to the cross. The church stood firm: Salvation is by grace alone.

That's why he asked Timothy to do something extreme—get circumcised—even though circumcision is not required for salvation. This might seem odd, especially since in Acts 15, the church council had just declared that circumcision isn't required for Gentiles to be saved. So, why did Paul circumcise Timothy?

Timothy is half Jewish, and everyone knew his father was Greek. Among Jews, Timothy's uncircumcision is a stumbling block. So Paul has him circumcised—not to please God but to avoid offending the very people they are trying to reach. As Paul wrote later in 1 Corinthians 9:20, "To the Jews I became like a Jew, to win the Jews." Paul isn't compromising the gospel; he is clearing the road for it. He asks Timothy to undergo circumcision—not for righteousness, but for mission.

Paul is crystal clear on the gospel. He is uncompromising in essentials, but astonishingly flexible in nonessentials. John Newton said Paul was "an iron pillar in essentials, and a reed in the wind on nonessentials."[8] Paul is willing to give up anything to make Jesus known.

So, how flexible are you? What are you willing to give up? What are you willing to do? We all like to think of ourselves as flexible, but our flexibility often has limits when it comes to things we enjoy. Paul is willing to do whatever it takes to proclaim a free gospel to anyone who would listen, including asking a young man to be circumcised so that the Jews would listen to him. What are you willing to do?

The Flexibility of a Famous Missionary

Hudson Taylor left England on September 19, 1853, under the Chinese Evangelization Society, and arrived in Shanghai on March 1, 1854. It didn't take long for him to notice a troubling pattern: Foreign missionaries were concentrated in coastal cities, far from the vast interior where millions had never heard of Jesus. When China's inland regions opened under British influence, Taylor saw the need firsthand—villages completely untouched by the gospel.

Eager to reach these unreached areas, he asked his mission agency for permission to go inland. When they refused, Taylor took a bold step. In 1865, he founded the China Inland Mission (now OMF International), devoted to bringing the gospel to China's heartland.

To remove cultural barriers, Taylor made a series of radical decisions. He grew out his hair, dyed it black, and wore traditional Chinese clothing, even adopting the appearance of a Chinese scholar. While other missionaries criticized him, Taylor's willingness to adapt opened doors. His approach bore fruit: By 1895, China Inland Mission had 641 missionaries—more than all other Protestant agencies in China combined.

Today, many missionaries follow his example, choosing cultural adaptation over comfort. Like Taylor, they lay down their preferences so others might hear the gospel without unnecessary obstacles.

Reflection

Paul and Timothy show us that radical flexibility with nonessentials can open doors for the gospel in surprising ways—just like Hudson Taylor adapting to Chinese culture. How might you be flexible so that others can more clearly see the beauty of his free grace?

DAY 40

THE EXAMPLE OF BRAND-NEW BELIEVERS

ACTS 17:6–7

"These men who have caused trouble all over the world have now come here, and Jason has welcomed them into his house. They are all defying Caesar's decrees, saying that there is another king, one called Jesus."

HAVE YOU ever considered brand-new believers to be people worth imitating? Usually not. We often view them as people who need to be discipled, not people who can serve in meaningful ways. The Thessalonians would like a word.

Paul and Silas stay briefly in Thessalonica, but their impact is so great that a mob rises against them and the new believers. Three accusations are brought against the missionaries in Thessalonica:

1. They have turned the world upside down.
2. Jason has shown them hospitality.
3. They are declaring Jesus as King.

Let's consider these charges carefully. From reading his letters to the Thessalonians, we know Paul teaches that Jesus will return and that God's kingdom will come. Declaring Jesus as King carries political implications, and obedience to Jesus takes precedence over obedience to Caesar.

The accusation that these missionaries "turned the world upside down" is striking. Essentially, they are being accused of treason. This is exactly what the gospel does—it transforms society at its core. It changes how Jews and Gentiles relate, redefines the value of men and women, and declares a King greater than Caesar. It's the implications of the gospel that stir things up. Social structures are transformed. Ethics are reshaped. Life decisions are altered. And the way people view their rulers is radically changed.

Jason, although not preaching himself, gets in trouble for offering hospitality. He may have been the first convert in Thessalonica, and it's likely the early church was meeting in his home. His guilt comes by association. In verse 8, we see the reaction:

> When they heard this, the crowd and the city officials were thrown into turmoil. Then they made Jason and the others post bond and let them go.

This isn't the end of the story for this church either, as Paul later writes them two letters. Consider the opening of 1 Thessalonians:

> You became imitators of us and of the Lord, for you welcomed the message in the midst of severe suffering with the joy given by the Holy Spirit. And so you became a model to all the believers in Macedonia and Achaia. (vv. 6–7)

Despite being only three months old, the Thessalonian church is already a model for other believers. Despite being so young in their faith, Paul praises them for their hospitality and perseverance amid suffering.

New believers should take note: Within three months of following Jesus, this church becomes a model for others. It's possible for young believers to lead the way and show what it looks like to follow Christ. Historically, many mission movements have been driven by young believers willing to take risks that older believers sometimes avoid.

How might your church be an example to other believers?

Turning Gaani Upside Down

How quickly can missionaries and new believers "turn the world upside down?"

Gaani is a small town of 3,200 people in Ghana, and I'm not sure even many Ghanaians know where it is. But Anthony and Dominic did, and they saw the need for a church plant there.

The town was filled with homes led by men who gathered to get drunk, only to return home and abuse their families. Wives and children were in desperate situations. Residents crafted rocks and iron into amulets to protect themselves from evil forces and to bring prosperity.

In April 2018, Anthony and Dominic moved into an abandoned building and began preaching the gospel. By November of that year, they had baptized forty-four people. Today, in a space that can comfortably seat fifty and uncomfortably fit seventy-five, they now welcome 106 regular attendees. The only solution is for church members and visitors to gather outside, crowding around the windows to catch a word from the preacher. Anthony and Dominic have turned Gaani upside down. And in just a very short time, they have become an example to Christians around the world.

Reflection

Are you holding younger believers back when they have so much to offer? How can you disciple them in such a way that they can be an example to people who have walked with Christ for decades?

DAY 41

STUDYING THE BIBLE WITHOUT BIBLES

ACTS 17:11–12

Now the Berean Jews were of more noble character than those in Thessalonica, for they received the message with great eagerness and examined the Scriptures every day to see if what Paul said was true. As a result, many of them believed, as did also a number of prominent Greek women and many Greek men.

"SEARCHING THE Scriptures" isn't just a Christian cliché—it's a vital posture of the heart. Whether we're wrestling with doubt, facing suffering, or simply longing to know God more deeply, we open the Bible not to check a box, but to seek a voice. That's why so many of us love the story of the Bereans in Acts 17. They don't just accept what they are told. They search the Scriptures daily to see if what Paul said was true. The word *searched* here carries a legal nuance—they cross-examine Paul's claims. But what if we've misunderstood what it really looked like for them to "search the Scriptures"?

If you've grown up in or around the church, you've probably heard this passage used as an example of how to be diligent in Scripture study. We are encouraged to "be like the Bereans," searching the Scriptures daily. If you search for sermons online, you'll find many on this very topic. However, I want to offer a new perspective on this passage—one that might challenge the way you've understood the Bereans.

The typical image we have is that the Bereans were sitting down with their Bibles, cross-referencing Paul's teachings with their own notes. Pastors often exhort us to follow their example, telling us to open our Bibles and verify what is preached. But there's a major point we overlook: the Bereans had no Bibles.

So, how did this work?

The Bereans gather daily in the synagogue, where Scripture is read aloud publicly. They discuss and debate it together. Many likely memorize large portions of Scripture, but they do not have the option of private study as we think of it today. Individual Bible reading is almost unheard of, since the majority of people are illiterate. As late as 1920, 80 percent of the world's population couldn't read. The concept of *quiet time* didn't emerge until the 1940s, popularized by InterVarsity in the United States.

When we think of "searching the Scriptures," we usually picture private study—reading the Bible alone, listening to a favorite online preacher, or reading a devotional book by ourselves. But that was not the case in the early church. Many of the Bereans likely couldn't read, and their engagement with Scripture was a communal, oral experience.

If we want to be true Bereans by searching the Scriptures, it won't be through solitary Bible study. Instead, it will be through studying and reflecting on Scripture together, in community. It will be testing what others say about the Scriptures together. The Christian faith, especially in its earliest days, was communal by nature. If we truly want to follow the Bereans' example, we should do so by engaging with Scripture in a shared, collective manner, not just by ourselves.

When you read about the Bereans, is your immediate reaction to go read the Bible by yourself? How might you follow their example by reading it with others?

Studying the Bible to Prove It Wrong

Esther grew up as a Muslim in Indonesia. She was incredibly religious—more religious than her other family members. She had a reputation in her community of being really serious about her faith. She used to think to herself, "I know many things in life will change, but one thing that will never change about me is I will always be Muslim." She was so religious she had even started applying to join jihadist groups.

One day, she thought she should improve her ability to poke holes in Christianity and somehow got her hands on a Bible. As she was reading it she couldn't help but think to herself, *Why is this better than the Quran? Why does this make so much more sense?* Even Revelation made so much sense to her!

After she read the Bible, she cried for three days straight. After that, she came out of her room and shocked her family by telling them that she had decided to follow the way of Jesus, rather than Muhammad. Now, she serves and shares Christ with Muslim minorities in Southern Thailand.

Reflection

The Bereans show us that genuine engagement with Scripture is deeply communal, marked by honest dialogue and a willingness to reconsider our assumptions. Who might God be prompting you to gather with to listen, question, and grow together in his Word?

DAY 42

UNDOING THE CULTURE'S STORY

ACTS 17:22–34

"The God who made the world and everything in it is the Lord of heaven and earth and does not live in temples built by human hands. And he is not served by human hands, as if he needed anything. Rather, he himself gives everyone life and breath and everything else." (17:24–25)

EVERY CULTURE has a story it tells to make sense of the world—heroes, major events, and festivals marking key moments. These shape our beliefs and identity.

Every culture also holds glimpses of truth about God but has missing pieces. Christianity retells the narrative to reveal that the gospel fulfills every culture's deepest longings, like the longings for purpose or the transcendent. Unlike Islam or Hinduism, which impose a specific culture, Christianity has a flexibility that both affirms and critiques cultural identities.

Paul's speech at Mars Hill in Acts 17 shows us this approach. Pulled before a gathering of Greek philosophers, he stands with the Acropolis towering above. Paul, with twenty years of missionary experience, doesn't water down the gospel but frames it within the listeners' worldview. He shares the story of God without references to Abraham, David, or Moses—figures his audience wouldn't recognize. Instead, he begins with what they know, affirming God as Creator and quoting their poets, showing them how the Lord in Christ answers the questions posed by their own religion.

When Peter preaches to Jews in Acts 2, he uses Bible terms because they know the scriptures. Similarly, in Acts 7, Stephen speaks of Jesus as the fulfillment of the Old Testament. Paul speaks to Jews in Acts 13 and refers to Old Testament stories. But in Acts 17, Paul's audience knows nothing of the faith, so he uses touchpoints from their culture.

When sharing the gospel, we need to be mindful of vocabulary, careful in how we explain the Christian faith, and intentional with entry points. How might you use the felt needs in your own culture to share the gospel?

Retelling a Culture's Mythology

In cultures that have never heard of Jesus, it's crucial to find cultural touchpoints as bridges to the gospel. Swedish missionaries Ola and Minnie Hanson did this with the Kachin people in Burma (modern-day Myanmar).

The Kachins had an extensive mythology, including stories of creation, death, resurrection, and a great flood. One story stood out—the tale of a lost book.

According to tradition, God gave every race a book: the Chinese received a book on paper, and the Burmese one on parchment. The Kachins, however, lost theirs when they ate it out of hunger on their way home.

The neighboring Karen people had a prophecy that one day a foreigner would return the lost book. When Ola Hanson heard this, he felt convicted to restore the lost book by translating the Bible into the Kachin language, fulfilling their ancient tradition and prophecy.

Reflection

We all carry stories in our hearts that define who we are and how we see the world, yet these stories inevitably fall short without Jesus at the center. Who might God be prompting you to engage with, using their own story as a bridge to share the good news?

DAY 43

PRISCILLA, AQUILA, AND APOLLOS

ACTS 18:24–26

Meanwhile a Jew named Apollos, a native of Alexandria, came to Ephesus. He was a learned man, with a thorough knowledge of the Scriptures. He had been instructed in the way of the Lord, and he spoke with great fervor and taught about Jesus accurately, though he knew only the baptism of John. He began to speak boldly in the synagogue. When Priscilla and Aquila heard him, they invited him to their home and explained to him the way of God more adequately.

HAVE YOU ever heard a gifted preacher but felt that something is just not quite right?

In Acts 18, we meet Apollos—a man who later shows up in Paul's letters to the Corinthians, and some even speculate he may have authored Hebrews (a good guess, though unconfirmed). Luke tells us he was a learned man, eloquent and powerful in speech. That might explain why some in Corinth are tempted to favor him over Paul (1 Corinthians 3:4).

But then we're told something curious: Apollos taught accurately about Jesus, yet he only knows the baptism of John. In other words, his theology is incomplete.

Not long after, Paul arrives in Ephesus—where Apollos had recently been—and discovers that the believers there also only knew John's baptism. They hadn't received Christian baptism or the Holy Spirit, likely due to Apollos's limited knowledge. Paul baptizes them in Jesus's name, and the Holy Spirit comes upon them.

So what exactly was going on with Apollos?

To teach about Jesus, Apollos must know of his death and resurrection. He clearly knows John the Baptist's message and testimony about the coming Messiah. But he didn't know about Pentecost or the outpouring of the Holy Spirit. It makes sense. If Apollos had been in Jerusalem after the resurrection but left before Pentecost, years might have passed without him hearing about what happened in Acts 2.

But then something beautiful happens. Priscilla and Aquila quietly take him aside. No public rebuke. No humiliation. They recognize that Apollos loves Jesus and has great potential as a teacher. He just needs help connecting the dots. So they guide him gently—likely with Priscilla taking the lead—and they help him grow in his understanding.

It's a beautiful picture of what it means to invest in future teachers.

Paul later speaks with admiration and affection for Apollos in 1 Corinthians 1–4. They weren't rivals—they were teammates in gospel ministry: "I planted the seed, Apollos watered it, but God has been making it grow" (1 Corinthians 3:6).

A Life Spent Strengthening the Church

I wish you could meet Uncle Monnie. I think he's traveled nearly four million miles in his lifetime, and everywhere he goes, he's beloved. I know because I've seen it firsthand. And though he's thirty years my senior, I can't keep up with him.

For more than forty years, he's been known to the persecuted church as their "American uncle"—a friend, pastor, and mentor. He's traveled to remote places, enduring grueling conditions, to train and encourage pastors in some of the world's hardest places to follow Christ. He remembers everyone he meets and treats them as equals and friends.

A few years ago, tens of thousands of Christians in Benue State, Nigeria, were attacked. Muslim militants killed men and children, burned villages, and destroyed fields. Thousands were displaced and now live in makeshift refugee camps—refugees in their own country. Most of the residents are widows and their children.

Monnie, along with a local pastor, visited those camps. He invited the pastors to join them for a week of training—six hours a day. He taught on "The Persecution of the Christian." You might think such a topic would deepen their despair. But it had the opposite effect. The response was electric. Nearly five hundred refugees packed four rooms each day, eager to learn. For many, it was their first time hearing what the Bible actually teaches about suffering for Christ.

Monnie is not a thrill-seeker. He's not driven by wanderlust. He is built by God to travel the world and strengthen the church. And like Priscilla and Aquila, he comes alongside leaders and helps them fill in the blanks of their theology.

Reflection

Some statistics suggest that 85 percent—or even up to 95 percent—of pastors outside the West have no formal training. But many are hungry to learn. Theological education is like a buffet: Western students often arrive already full, but pastors outside the West come with empty plates. They have never read a Christian book nor owned a commentary.

We've been given a gift—training, access, mobility. Pray that more people will step in to help—like Priscilla and Aquila, like Uncle Monnie—to strengthen the church where it's growing fast and under fire.

DAY 44

RELENTLESS MINISTRY

ACTS 19

While Apollos was at Corinth, Paul took the road through the interior and arrived at Ephesus. (19:1)

IT'S NOW AD 54, more than twenty years after Jesus's death and resurrection and the coming of the Holy Spirit in Jerusalem. Paul enters the synagogue in Ephesus—his standard approach wherever he goes. His heart has always been for the Jew first. For three months, he debates about the kingdom of God.

This period is longer than any other synagogue ministry during Paul's travels. He engages in three activities: speaking boldly, reasoning, and persuading. This is a dynamic exchange—a dialogue. His central message? The kingdom of God, a theological shorthand for God's rule established through Jesus. Paul proclaims Jesus as the fulfillment of all things.

He shifts his efforts to the hall of Tyrannus. Acts 19:9–10 records that for two years, Paul conducts daily discussions there. Because of this relentless effort, Luke says that "all the residents of Asia heard the word of the Lord" (v. 10).

Paul's daily schedule likely goes like this: manual labor in the morning, teaching and debating during the midday siesta, and returning to work at night. This routine—day after day, six days a week—continues for two years. Why the middle of the day? Because it is siesta time, and the hall is available. While others rest, Paul seizes the opportunity to teach—relentlessly.

Paul takes the gospel public. He trusts it can withstand scrutiny, debate, and ridicule. For two years, he pours himself out for the gospel, tirelessly. Remember, he is single and has control over his time. But consider the resolve: he works to ensure no one can accuse him of preaching for profit. Where's the leisure? The breaks? The vacation? None are recorded for us. We live in a culture that loves comfort and flexibility. Let's remember Paul's dedication to the Ephesians—preaching while others rested. Let's reflect on his determination to spread the gospel, even in challenging circumstances.

Nonstop Church Planting

From 2005 to 2010, Mohsen was involved in a movement that planted forty-eight churches in twenty cities across Iran. But on December 26, 2010, he and many of his fellow pastors were arrested, charged with "acts against national security through evangelism." He spent five years in prison. During one of those years Mohsen spent 361 consecutive days in solitary confinement, not seeing the sun for almost a full year. Yet, he testified, "The Lord was my light and my salvation."

Recounting the story, Mohsen said, "Suffering and persecution are not the end of the story; they are part of the story." Today, many believe that Iran has the fastest-growing church in the world.

Reflection

Paul's unrelenting labor in the hall of Tyrannus illustrates a gospel that refuses to sit idle—even when scorned or opposed. In the same way, the power of Jesus can break the darkest strongholds, transforming lives once bound by the most desperate practices. Where might God be inviting you to such steadfast, public witness in your own sphere of influence?

DAY 45

ENCOUNTERING THE DEMONIC

ACTS 19:11–16

One day the evil spirit answered them, "Jesus I know, and Paul I know about, but who are you?" (19:15)

SOMETIMES, I receive mail with offers like, "Send me fifteen dollars for blessed water from the Jordan River," or "Send twenty-five dollars for a blessed napkin." In almost every one of these offers, the focus is on the evangelist, often raising money for their luxurious lifestyle, while Jesus takes a back seat. These televangelists resemble the first-century magicians more than anything else.

In Ephesus, Paul isn't primarily known for a healing ministry. Luke even calls these healings "extraordinary" because they are unexpected. People use Paul's work clothes to heal others, just as Peter's shadow heals people and Jesus heals someone when they simply touches his robe. These miracles aren't about Paul or something he is selling; they are God's work, validating Paul's apostolic ministry. There's a significant difference between this and what we see in modern times, where "healing" is often commodified. Paul isn't profiting from these miracles—he works and teaches for free six days a week.

The healings are followed by some of the funniest stories in the book of Acts. First-century exorcists invoke a name they believe is more powerful than the spirit they are dealing with. They don't care about knowing Jesus—they just want to use his name as a tool, a magic formula for success.

The seven sons of Sceva do exactly this, saying to a possessed man, "In the name of the Jesus whom Paul preaches, I command you to come out" (v. 13). The demon responds, "Jesus I know, and Paul I know about, but who are you?" (v. 15).

What a chilling response. A demon looks at you and says, "I know Jesus, but who are you?" Jesus is known because he commands even the demons. Paul is known too, because he is fighting against the kingdom of darkness. If you're making an impact in spiritual warfare, the demons will know your name. It should be our goal to be known in this way—for advancing the kingdom of God and standing against darkness.

The sons of Sceva, however, treat Jesus's name like a charm or talisman, like a lucky coin or superstition. They have no real understanding of the power they are trying to invoke. As a result, the demon overpowers them, and they end up running down the street, naked and bleeding—humiliated and reduced to a joke. They become the seven streaking sons of Sceva.

In your life, how do you use the name of Jesus? Is he just an impersonal force you call on to get what you want? Or is he the Lord of the universe and Savior of your soul? Is he your passion, or merely part of your magic act? Do you say to Jesus, "Follow me, I've got this"? Or are you centering your life on him, recognizing that he rescues you from sin and death? The gospel is a public declaration of power—God's power. And when we truly understand that, it changes everything.

In the Name of Jesus?

A new Christian from the Middle East once shared with me, "Americans can come here, start a ministry, and become very wealthy. There is a significant market here for ministry and money." How does this happen?

One woman told me about hearing about a particular ministry in the city that was known for issuing baptism certificates quickly. Smugglers had even informed them that if they wanted to enter the United Kingdom, they needed to claim they had become Christians and would require some kind of proof.

For two weeks, she told people she was a Christian, though she had no real understanding of what that meant. The ministry gathered a group of twenty-five people—none of whom were true believers, as she later realized when their names appeared in a letter raising support. "We joked about it before and after the baptisms," she said. "I wanted to be baptized first, just so I wouldn't have to step into cold water after everyone else. It was freezing, and I got sick for two weeks. But everyone received a baptism certificate to present to the authorities."

Interestingly, the woman who shared her story with me did become a Christian a few months later.

Sometimes ministries spend all their time telling the stories of impact with the intention of just fundraising. There is a better way. It's not built on numbers or narratives crafted to impress donors, but on truth-telling, discipleship, and genuine community. It's slow, often unseen, and rarely marketable. But it's real. The better way values integrity over image, people over performance. It resists shortcuts that exploit broken systems and instead walks the long road of faith formation.

Reflection

When God works powerfully, it's never a product to be bought or sold, but an invitation to trust Jesus as Lord of all. In what ways might you be tempted to use Jesus's name for your own ends rather than bowing before him as King?

DAY 46

BURNING THE SAFETY NETS

ACTS 19:19–20

A number who had practiced sorcery brought their scrolls together and burned them publicly. When they calculated the value of the scrolls, the total came to fifty thousand drachmas. In this way the word of the Lord spread widely and grew in power.

ARE YOU still holding on to remnants of your life before you knew Jesus? The call to follow Christ really is a call to let go of everything else you've ever relied on for security, identity, and belonging. It is a total surrender by faith that Jesus can save and satisfy.

A revival breaks out in Ephesus among Jews and Greeks. Many new believers, still holding onto remnants of their former lives, came to a point of public confession. They likely keep their magical scrolls as a safety net, unsure whether their new faith in Jesus is sufficient. But they soon realize they need to rely entirely on God, which leads them to confess their past practices and turn fully to Christ.

In a dramatic act of devotion, they gather their magical scrolls and burn them publicly. The value of these scrolls is estimated at around 50,000 drachmas—a drachma being roughly equivalent to a day's wage. To put it in modern terms, that could be around $2.5 million. The burning of the scrolls marks a definitive choice: Either Christ has power, or their magic does. This act results in what may be one of the most expensive bonfires in history and a powerful testimony to the transforming work of God.

The Ephesian Christians probably don't see the problem right away when they first believe. It takes a dramatic event—seven men running naked and bleeding down the street—to open their eyes to the truth. Look at the impact outside the Christian community: "In this way the word of the Lord spread widely and grew in power" (v. 20).

The impact on Ephesus comes from Christians confessing their sins, renouncing them publicly, and sacrificing valuable possessions to show their devotion to Christ. The watching world sees this and thinks, "They must truly believe this."

What would that look like in your life?

Are there things you're still holding on to—habits, relationships, comforts, or identities—that reveal a lingering doubt that Jesus is truly enough? Maybe it's not a scroll, but it *is* something you turn to for a sense of control, comfort, or worth. What's your safety net?

A Bigger Power, A Stronger Hope

The transformation of the once-jungled land where a seminary now stands is a testament to God's power to redeem what was once a symbol of enslavement to the worship of spirits. An African leader needed a location for his dream of training pastors, and he found a plot on the outskirts of Monrovia, Liberia. The land was corporately owned by the community and sold at a low price because it was believed to be demon-possessed.

The two-acre plot had three large trees considered sacred, used in animistic ceremonies for young women. Female shamans performed rituals, including female genital mutilation, binding the women to spirits believed to dwell in the trees. The trees were stained with the blood from these rituals, and the community feared that if the trees were removed, the women would die, and disaster would strike. This belief led them to sell the land cheaply, thinking the school would fail.

But the Christians bought the land, confidently proclaiming their confidence that God was bigger than the spiritual power the community believed in. The animistic community leaders waited with bated breath for this Christian endeavor to crash and burn. However, the church prayed over the land, asking for God's protection and blessing. Then, they cut and burned the trees and began building.

The community watched, expecting judgment to fall. But the days passed. No women died. No calamity came. Instead, classrooms rose from the soil. A primary school opened. A seminary took shape. And from that place, the Word of the Lord began to spread.

Just like in Ephesus, where scrolls were burned and the power of Jesus was made visible, the people saw something unmistakable: God is greater. Greater than spirits. Greater than fear. Greater than the things they once hoped in.

From this the Word of God spread.

Reflection

God's power was so real and undeniable in Ephesus that new believers were compelled to discard their former ways at great personal cost. So, we must ask ourselves: what are our modern-day sacred security blankets that God is asking us to let go of and to trust Jesus instead? How does the gospel transform our source of hope and well-being?

DAY 47

A CHANGE OF PLANS

ACTS 19:21–22

After all this had happened, Paul decided to go
to Jerusalem, passing through Macedonia and Achaia.
"After I have been there," he said, "I must visit Rome also."
He sent two of his helpers, Timothy and Erastus,
to Macedonia, while he stayed in the province of Asia
a little longer.

HAS GOD ever interrupted your plans or changed your mind?

Maybe you mapped out your future clearly—career, relationships, ministry—but then something happened. A door closed. A crisis hit. A new opportunity arose. Suddenly, the path you were so sure of taking took a turn you didn't expect.

That's exactly what happens in this seemingly small transition in Acts 19. Luke writes that "after all this had happened, Paul decided to go to Jerusalem," passing through Macedonia and Achaia first. But these aren't just logistical updates—they mark a pivotal shift in Paul's ministry, setting the course for the rest of the book of Acts.

Around the same time, Paul writes the letter we know as 1 Corinthians. Notice how Acts 19 parallels Paul's words at the end of 1 Corinthians 16:

> After I go through Macedonia, I will come to you—for I will be going through Macedonia. Perhaps I will stay with

> you for a while, or even spend the winter, so that you can help me on my journey, wherever I go. For I do not want to see you now and make only a passing visit; I hope to spend some time with you, if the Lord permits. But I will stay on at Ephesus until Pentecost, because a great door for effective work has opened to me, and there are many who oppose me. (1 Corinthians 16:5–9)

Luke, the author of Acts, doesn't mention the change of plans that leads Paul to consider returning to Corinth, but Paul evidently makes adjustments. Then, he changes his plans again:

> I wanted to visit you first so that you might benefit twice. I wanted to visit you on my way to Macedonia and to come back to you from Macedonia, and then to have you send me on my way to Judea. Was I fickle when I intended to do this? Or do I make my plans in a worldly manner so that in the same breath I say both "Yes, yes" and "No, no"? (2 Corinthians 1:15–17)

Paul's defense shows something real: People misunderstand him. They question his reliability. Ministry isn't clean and predictable. Life happens. And in 2 Corinthians 1:8–9, Paul admits that he and Timothy had gone through so much hardship that they had "despaired of life itself," but that it was so they would not rely on themselves but on God, who raises the dead.

So yes—plans change. But so does Paul. God uses the interruption to deepen Paul's dependence and shift the course of his mission.

Acts 19:21–22 might feel like a travel update, but it's a reminder that God is always guiding—even through closed doors, detours, and disappointments.

Is there an area where your plans didn't go as expected? How might God be using that to reorient your heart or redirect your steps? God's interruptions are not obstacles—they're often invitations.

God's Redirect

Several years ago, my friend was walking down the street in a European city when he passed a ministry. He suddenly felt as though the Lord was speaking directly to him, urging him to go upstairs and talk to his friend Mike about the idea that Muslims would soon begin pouring into the city. Though it seemed improbable, he decided to turn around and see if Mike was there.

To his surprise, Mike was indeed there. As soon as they saw each other, Mike said, "Hey, I was just talking about you with my friend." Without hesitation, my friend responded, "Would you be willing to attend a conference with me? I believe Muslims are going to start arriving, and we need to be prepared."

Mike smiled and said, "That's funny. I was just discussing this very topic with my friend moments ago. Let's do it."

This conversation led to several ministries coming together to discuss how best to reach Muslims—just before the refugee crisis unfolded in Europe in 2015.

Reflection

Paul's shifting travel plans reveal that even the greatest servants of Christ must sometimes adjust course when faced with life's twists and turns. Where might God be inviting you to hold your plans loosely, trusting him to redirect you toward a greater purpose than you first imagined?

DAY 48

FRIENDS IN MINISTRY

ACTS 20:4

He was accompanied by Sopater son of Pyrrhus from Berea, Aristarchus and Secundus from Thessalonica, Gaius from Derbe, Timothy also, and Tychicus and Trophimus from the province of Asia.

MINISTRY IS not a solo journey. Even the apostle Paul doesn't go it alone. In Acts 20, we're given a list of names that might seem like a quick travel note—but look closer, and you'll see something deeply important: Friendship and partnership are essential to Paul's ministry.

I've traveled a lot, and certain names—partners in the gospel—carry rich meaning for me. Just thinking about them brings back stories, laughter, tears, and the shared weight of mission. Paul's companions are more than assistants—they are brothers. Each name here tells a story of faith, sacrifice, and unity in Christ.

Take Aristarchus and Secundus from Thessalonica. Aristarchus is likely from a noble family; his name suggests high status. But alongside him is Secundus—literally, "Second." That's not just a name; it's a reminder of social class. In the Roman world, slaves were often given numerical names: Tertius ("Third"), Quartus ("Fourth"), and so on. Yet here in this band of missionaries, status doesn't divide. The gospel has united people who otherwise would never have stood side by side.

In fact, in Romans 16, we meet Tertius—another likely slave—who writes down the letter to the Romans. He even signs his name. Think about that: A man without legal personhood is the one to pen one of the most theologically rich letters in Christian history.

These names aren't filler. They're friends. They're partners. They represent churches standing together in mission. These men carry offerings from their churches to help the struggling believers in Jerusalem. They aren't just supporting Paul—they are joining him. And the fact that they are all Gentiles must have been purposeful. Paul wants to give the struggling Jerusalem church a visual expression of the impact of the gospel by bringing his Gentile friends to give financial support to the Jewish Christians.

True Christian friendship doesn't ignore differences. It transcends them. In Christ, the barriers that divide us—race, class, background—are broken down. Ministry becomes a shared labor, not a platform for one but a partnership among many. Ministry without friendship is lonely. But when we walk together—across backgrounds and burdens—we bear witness to a better kingdom.

Are your friendships shaped by the gospel in such a way that they reflect the unity, diversity, and mutual sacrifice of these early believers?

Give Us Friends

In 1910, 1,200 representatives from a wide range of churches and missionary societies gathered in Edinburgh, Scotland, for the World Missionary Conference. The goal of the conference was the evangelization of the world within the lifetime of those attending.

Of note was that very few non-Westerners were featured as plenary speakers. One who did was Bishop Vendanayagam Samuel Azariah. He famously concluded his speech with these words:

> Through all the ages to come, the Indian church will rise up in gratitude to attest the heroism and self-denying labors of the missionary body. You have given your goods to feed the poor. You have given your bodies to be burned. We also ask for love. Give us FRIENDS.[9]

Global Christianity was still dominated by Western leaders hesitant to give up leadership. "Worldwide Christianity" at the time meant missions from Europe and North America to the rest of the world. Azariah, speaking for the global church, wanted friendship. He wanted equality. He wanted to be treated as an equal.

The Western church was celebrating the impact of the gospel around the world. But they needed the gospel to impact their own friendships—to, like Paul, see people from other cultures and backgrounds and co-laborers and equals.

Reflection

The early church was a living tapestry, where slaves and nobles traveled side by side for the sake of the gospel, demolishing every barrier the Roman world had erected. Who in your life might God be inviting you to embrace as a friend and equal, despite any societal labels that say otherwise?

DAY 49

TEACHING THROUGH THE NIGHT

ACTS 20:7–11

On the first day of the week we came together to break bread. Paul spoke to the people and, because he intended to leave the next day, kept on talking until midnight. There were many lamps in the upstairs room where we were meeting. Seated in a window was a young man named Eutychus, who was sinking into a deep sleep as Paul talked on and on. When he was sound asleep, he fell to the ground from the third story and was picked up dead. Paul went down, threw himself on the young man and put his arms around him. "Don't be alarmed," he said. "He's alive!" Then he went upstairs again and broke bread and ate After talking until daylight, he left.

THE STORY of Eutychus is well known. Poor Eutychus. His name is forever associated with falling asleep in church. Every Christian who has read or heard Acts will one day meet Eutychus and know what happened to him.

The American way of interpreting this is primarily reading it as humor. Either it's Paul's fault for being long-winded, or it's Eutychus's fault—and we can all laugh, because everyone has fallen asleep in church at some point. And you might even be pulled to criticize Paul, because our culture tends to laugh and poke fun at people in authority. But I think our view of poking fun at authority figures as a culture lends us to see a different point about the text than Luke is trying to make.

Luke does not speak positively of sleep. Only he gives us a specific detail in the story of Jesus taking Peter, James, and John onto a mountain to pray. While Jesus prays, his appearance transfigures, and he speaks of his departure. The disciples, however, are weighed down with sleep (Luke 9:32). The same terminology found in Luke 9:32 appears again when sleep weighs down upon Eutychus in Acts 20:9.

Luke also highlights the disciples' tendency to fall asleep at night when they should be praying and staying alert—most prominently in Luke 22:39–46. Jesus twice instructs his disciples to pray that they might not come into the time of trial (22:40, 46). Yet, the disciples fail miserably by falling asleep at an important moment rather than praying. They fall asleep on a night when they should remain vigilant.

The story is not just about sleep. It seems like an afterthought. Eutychus falls, but then Paul runs down and wraps his arms around him. And immediately Eutychus is healed (or raised from the dead, depending on how you read it!). But then look what happens. Paul and the Christians go right back to teaching and the breaking of bread. I want you to marvel that they just go right back to a worship service. The falling asleep and healing was not what was most important. It almost reads like a blip in the story.

Paul teaches until daylight. He just keeps going. The miracle was important enough to mention, but the core of the gathering of Christians was teaching and sharing of meals, and most likely one meal in particular, the Lord's Supper.

We are all drawn to miraculous stories. They are wonderful. But this story pushes us to see how much Paul valued teaching and fellowship. How might you rightly order the value of teaching and miracles? What brings you more comfort?

When Miracles Aren't the Main Thing

I was once walking with my friend Javad. Over the years he had told me several stories of God's miraculous work among the Iranians he shared the gospel with and the church he pastored. They were always overwhelming. But one day, as we walked, I had to help him to remember some of the stories—they just weren't on the front of his mind as he moved forward in proclaiming the gospel. He then turned to me with a smile and said, "These happen all the time. I just can't remember them all."

For him, the miracles were not ultimate. He was not trying to make money off of them or put himself forward as a miracle worker. Jesus was ultimate. And that is what he wanted to talk about.

Reflection

Even amid miracles like Eutychus's dramatic fall and healing, the early church kept returning to what mattered most—Christ-centered teaching and shared fellowship. In a culture dazzled by the extraordinary, how can you guard against spiritual drowsiness and keep Jesus at the center of your worship and service?

DAY 50

A GOSPEL GOODBYE

ACTS 20:17–38

When Paul had finished speaking, he knelt down with all of them and prayed. They all wept as they embraced him and kissed him. What grieved them most was his statement that they would never see his face again. Then they accompanied him to the ship. (20:36–38)

THE BIBLE is filled with goodbyes. Jacob says goodbye to his sons. Moses says goodbye. David says goodbye. Jesus says goodbye to his disciples. And then there's a significant goodbye in Acts 20, perhaps the most emotional farewell in the entire book of Acts.

Have you ever been part of a purposeful goodbye? Maybe it was a family member who was dying and wanted to say goodbye. If you're the one saying farewell, especially in a moment like that, you carefully weigh your words. You think deeply about what you're going to say. Or consider the moment you drop someone off at college, or when you're dropped off yourself. If the relationship is meaningful, tears will likely flow. What is said in those final moments carries immense weight.

Acts 20 captures one of the most heartfelt goodbyes in the Bible. The apostle Paul isn't just a saint to be revered or a prolific writer. He isn't simply an evangelist. He's a human being with deep friendships. He's not a robot; he's a man full of emotion. Take a look at the end of this chapter:

> When Paul had finished speaking, he knelt down with all of them and prayed. They all wept as they embraced him and kissed him. What grieved them most was his statement that they would never see his face again. Then they accompanied him to the ship. (20:36–38)

This was a goodbye to friends. It's not something we see in other places in Acts. When Paul launches from Antioch, there is no mention of this kind of emotional farewell—they know they will see him again. This isn't the response in Philippi, Thessalonica, Athens, or Corinth either. But in Ephesus, the city where Paul labors the longest, the city he loves, the response is different.

Paul is passing by Ephesus. He doesn't go directly to the city but stops thirty miles away in Miletus. He sends for the elders from Ephesus, knowing it would take time—perhaps a two-day journey back and forth—but he wants to see them. And they come. Paul delivers his farewell sermon, knowing it will be his final goodbye.

It's also important to note that this is the only recorded speech in Acts directed specifically to Christians. While Paul certainly speaks to Christians at other times—like in the earlier verses of this chapter—those words aren't recorded. Here, however, we get a glimpse into how Paul speaks to believers. Every other speech in Acts is evangelistic in nature, delivered to unbelieving Gentiles, Jews, or as part of his legal defenses in the coming chapters. But here, we have a window into Paul's words to the church, giving us insight into his heart for his fellow believers.

Can you recall times you have had to say goodbye for the sake of the gospel? One of the hidden costs of sending missionaries is to the grandparents of the kids of missionaries, who say goodbye to their grandchildren for the sake of gospel work. Take a moment to pray for them and imagine what they must feel.

Saying Goodbye

The hardest goodbye I've ever been part of was watching my friend bid farewell to an Eritrean church in Europe that he had faithfully served for over twenty years. During that time, he baptized hundreds and discipled many others. To make ends meet, he also worked long hours as a jeweler.

Now with a wife and young child to care for, the country he called home offered him no realistic prospect for economic survival. There was no future for him and his family in that place. Thankfully, Canada had extended its hand of mercy, granting asylum to him and his loved ones. And so, there he stood at the pulpit, weeping as he said goodbye to the community he loved so dearly.

When he arrived in Toronto, he was greeted by one of the men he had discipled, who was now the pastor of the Eritrean church there.

Reflection

Love and tears show that God's family is bound by more than a mission statement; it's a bond forged by grace and nurtured through shared life. Who in your life might God be calling you to treasure in such a way that goodbyes are difficult?

DAY 51

VISITING THE CHURCHES PAUL "PLANTED"

ACTS 21

After sighting Cyprus and passing to the south of it, we sailed on to Syria. We landed at Tyre, where our ship was to unload its cargo. We sought out the disciples there and stayed with them seven days. (21:3–4)

WHEN WE read Acts slowly and thoughtfully, we start to notice something remarkable: The gospel is often carried forward not through strategy or planning, but through suffering and disruption. Scattered believers—ordinary Christians displaced by hardship—play a crucial role in planting the very churches Paul visits later in his ministry.

The first stop on Paul's journey to Jerusalem is Tyre (vv. 3–4). But how did the gospel reach Tyre? As far as we know, Paul has never visited, and the disciples there have never met him. The answer actually comes from Acts 11.

> Now those who had been scattered by the persecution that broke out when Stephen was killed traveled as far as Phoenicia, Cyprus, and Antioch. (11:19)

Tyre is in Phoenicia, and it is unknown Christians, scattered by persecution, who carry the gospel there. Ironically, it is Paul himself, before his conversion, who is responsible for scattering them. You could say Paul "plants" this church—though not through intentional missionary efforts, but by persecuting Christians before he met Christ and was transformed. In a sense, Paul plants churches even before his conversion! That's how God works.

Luke, who is traveling with Paul, likely asks the believers in Tyre, "How did the gospel reach you?" They probably reply, "It came through those who were scattered by the persecution caused by Paul," and that small note makes its way into Acts 11:19. Paul had driven believers to Phoenicia, and now he stays with them. He had pushed believers to Cyprus—the same people he meets on his first missionary journey. And he had scattered believers to Antioch, the church he later pastors and is sent out from. This should make you marvel at how God works, even through the enemy's plans.

Imagine how these people could have reacted to Paul! Mnason opens his home to him (21:16)! Back in Tyre, they kneel and pray together on the beach (21:5). It's a beautiful display of forgiveness and grace. God weaves together these improbable stories.

Maybe you know someone whose life once stood in opposition to the gospel but has now been transformed by it. What would it look like to follow the example of these early believers—people who not only forgive but embrace their former enemy as family in Christ?

Displaced but Not Defeated

The movement of people will be a defining factor in the next one hundred years—not only for Christian missions but for the world at large.

Take the story of Hassan, for example. Coming to Christ from a Syrian Orthodox background, he pursued theological training and served in Lebanon for many years. He eventually planted a church in Aleppo, Syria, and faithfully pastored it for twelve years, until 2015, when the church building was destroyed by a bombing. He and his wife were forced to flee, becoming refugees in

Canada, while his entire congregation was scattered throughout Europe.

Despite these challenges, Hassan and his dispersed congregation have planted new churches across Europe. Today, he dedicates his time to traveling back to the Middle East to train pastors and leaders, continuing to strengthen the church in some of the most difficult regions in the world.

A bombing led to church planting.

Reflection

The people who are scattered will be a dominant force in missions over the next one hundred years. Take time to pray for scattered Christians around the world as they bring the gospel with them.

DAY 52

AM I DOING ENOUGH?

ACTS 21:8–9

Leaving the next day, we reached Caesarea and stayed at the house of Philip the evangelist, one of the Seven. He had four unmarried daughters who prophesied.

I LOVE how some stories come full circle. When reading Acts, I often wonder: What is everyone else doing? Where is Peter? Where is James? What happened to the apostles? Did any of them settle down? Did they have families? Were they married? Well, we get an answer to some of those questions in this passage, through the person of Philip.

Let's remind ourselves who Philip is. In Acts 6:5, he is one of the seven chosen to oversee the care of the poor in Jerusalem. But then, an entire chapter is devoted to him and his missionary work. In Acts 8, we read of his ministry that arises because of persecution caused by Paul. And then, Philip disappears from the narrative—until this passage, twenty-eight years later.

Not everyone is Paul. Sometimes we read Acts as though we are supposed to be just like Paul or his companions, and a sneaky kind of guilt sets in—*Am I doing enough?* Reading Paul's life can make us feel exhausted just thinking about everything he did. But here's Philip. We don't know anything about his ministry after Acts 8, and his story isn't as flashy or extensive as Paul's. Now, Philip is older—likely in his late forties or early fifties. He's been living in

Caesarea, is married, and is raising four daughters, all of whom have the gift of prophecy. Philip has settled down and committed his life to Jesus in a different way. God gives each of us a unique life—married or single, with children or without. Some of us are more able-bodied than others. Some have different capacities. We are who God made us to be, and we can rest in that.

Interestingly, Philip's initial departure from Jerusalem is catalyzed by the persecution led by Paul—yet here he is decades later, faithfully serving in a quieter role, hosting Paul and his travel companions. His life shows that God can move us into new arenas of ministry for a season and then settle us into places where our obedience may seem less dramatic but is no less important. Sometimes, like Philip, we're called to put down roots, raise a family, and serve God right where we are—no less faithful, just different.

The 3 × 300 Movement

The gospel was brought to Myanmar (formerly Burma) through the tireless efforts of Adoniram Judson, a pioneering missionary. In 1819, Judson baptized his first convert, an event that filled him with hope. He famously wrote:

> O may it prove the beginning of a series of baptisms in the Burman Empire which shall continue in uninterrupted succession to the end of time!

In 1978, the Kachin Baptist Convention embarked on a significant missionary endeavor, recruiting three hundred people to carry the gospel message. These individuals underwent forty days of training before being sent out in teams for a three-year commitment—hence it was called the 3 × 300 Movement. I first heard of this while standing before a commemorative statue bearing the names of all three hundred missionaries. One of them, a Christian leader named Hkalam Samson, was beside me, sharing his story.

Hkalam was recently imprisoned on charges of terrorism, unlawful association, and inciting opposition—charges that anyone who knows him would find absurd.

As we stood there, Hkalam pointed to a name on the statue and said, "That man was raised from the dead after being stoned. You can go visit him if you like." I was astonished. Yet, as incredible as that miracle was, what truly mattered was the preaching of the gospel and the resulting conversions. It's believed that up to 6,200 converts were baptized in one day—perhaps the largest baptismal service in church history.

And forty years later, you can find many of those who committed to this ministry in towns across Myanmar. Like Philip, they settled down, had families, and worked quietly in their local churches. No great revival has happened since, but God's faithfulness remains evident.

Reflection

Where might God be inviting you to embrace the unique place and season he has you in, trusting that your settled life can still be a powerful witness to his grace?

DAY 53
TO JERUSALEM
ACTS 21:12–14

When we heard this, we and the people there pleaded with Paul not to go up to Jerusalem. Then Paul answered, "Why are you weeping and breaking my heart? I am ready not only to be bound, but also to die in Jerusalem for the name of the Lord Jesus." When he would not be dissuaded, we gave up and said, "The Lord's will be done."

PAUL IS compelled to go to Jerusalem. With him are Gentile converts and money from Gentile churches for the Jewish Christians. But his friends know it will be dangerous.

They are worried they will lose Paul, are worried about his suffering, and are expressing genuine love for him. Luke is among those weeping. Wouldn't you feel the same way? They don't want to lose Paul. Their motives are not selfish or wrong—they stem from love.

In the end, Paul is following his Savior, turning toward Jerusalem, knowing suffering awaits him. In his Gospel, Luke writes, "Jesus resolutely set out for Jerusalem" (Luke 9:51). Now, Luke tells a similar story about Paul:

> Then Paul answered, "Why are you weeping and breaking my heart? I am ready not only to be bound but also to die in Jerusalem for the name of the Lord Jesus." When he

> would not be dissuaded, we gave up and said, "The Lord's will be done" (21:13–14).

Read those words again: "I am ready."

Many of you know of Pastor Tim Keller. As he was nearing death, his son Michael shared some of his final words. Here's what he said:

> I'm thankful for all the people who've prayed for me over the years. I'm thankful for my family that loves me. I'm thankful for the time God has given me, but I am ready to see Jesus. I can't wait to see Jesus. Send me home.[10]

Do you hear it? "I am ready."

Paul acknowledges that his friends are trying to break his resolve. He doesn't chastise them for it. He understands their tears. But he simply says, "I am ready." And then his friends respond with, "The Lord's will be done."

Isn't that the prayer we all want? God's will be done, no matter what. Is there a situation right now in your life where you know difficulty will lie ahead if you follow what God has for you, but you are resolute to say, "I am ready"? What about when a friend faces difficulty based on a decision they think the Lord wants them to make? Will you try and hold them back, or say, with tears, "The Lord's will be done"?

Difficulty Should Not Hold You Back

One common reason people discourage others from going into missions is that it will be "too hard." It was George Verwer, the late founder of Operation Mobilization, who said something like, "There are no such things as closed countries. All of them are open to get into; they just might be closed on the way out."

There's a story of a one-legged schoolteacher from Scotland who came to Hudson Taylor, offering himself as a missionary to

China. Some believed it would be too hard for him—and certainly not God's will. Taylor asked him, "With only one leg, why do you think of going as a missionary?" The teacher, George Scott, replied, "I do not see those with two legs going, so I must."[11]

He was accepted.

Reflection

As you reflect on Paul's words, "I am ready," and the courage it takes to walk into difficulty for the sake of Christ, take time to pray for those today who are facing a high cost for their obedience to the Great Commission. Let your heart be shaped by their stories, and intercede with boldness and compassion.

Pray for pastors, missionaries, and believers in places like Afghanistan, Iran, North Korea, and Syria who face prison, violence, or death for their faith. Ask God to give them the courage of Paul—to be ready not only to suffer but even to die for the name of the Lord Jesus. Ask the Lord to help you say, "I am ready," in whatever he calls you to.

DAY 54

REPORTING WHAT GOD HAS DONE

ACTS 21:17–19

When we arrived at Jerusalem, the brothers and sisters received us warmly. The next day Paul and the rest of us went to see James, and all the elders were present. Paul greeted them and reported in detail what God had done among the Gentiles through his ministry.

THE BELIEVERS in Jerusalem warmly receive Paul. The next day, he immediately goes to meet with the elders, including James. James is the leader of the Jerusalem church—the same James who wrote the letter of James, the half brother of Jesus and the one who declared in Acts 15 that Gentiles could be Christians without becoming Jews first. Along with him are the elders, the leaders of the Jerusalem church.

Paul isn't alone—he has Gentile believers with him, living examples of what God has been doing. He reports in detail all that God has done among the Gentiles, and James and the elders rejoice.

> Paul greeted them and reported in detail what God had done among the Gentiles through his ministry. (v. 19)

This isn't the first time Paul has given such a report. He did in Acts 15:12 as well:

> The whole assembly became silent as they listened to Barnabas and Paul telling about the signs and wonders God had done among the Gentiles through them.

Notice the emphasis: what God has done.

This is a critical point to drive into our hearts and minds. There's something within us that loves to take credit for success. Certainly, couldn't Paul take credit? Look at how hard he worked, how far he traveled, and what he endured. But in the end, Paul's report is not about his achievements; it is about what God has done.

Have you ever seen reconciliation among Christians? God did it. Have you seen someone come to faith? God did it. Have you experienced radical change in your own life? God did it. Are you skilled at something? God did it. This is what Paul writes in 1 Corinthians 4:7:

> For who makes you different from anyone else? What do you have that you did not receive? And if you did receive it, why do you boast as though you did not?

Why do the authors of the Bible continually remind us of this? Because we are prone to take credit. Paul reminds us, "Let the one who boasts boast in the Lord" (2 Corinthians 10:17). And that's what Paul is doing here. He gives a detailed report of what God has done.

In both Acts 15 and 21, Paul tells stories. He probably told of Sergius Paulus and how they blinded the Jewish sorcerer. Or the signs and wonders in Iconium. Or the healing of a man born lame in Lystra. Or how they were worshipped by mistake. Or the stoning he endured. Or their circling back to the same towns to strengthen the disciples.

And now in Acts 21, imagine Paul recounting the riot in Ephesus and the burning of scrolls by people who were converted. There are so many stories filled with God's work.

Human beings are not made to be worshipped. We are meant to stir others to worship God. There is freedom in writing yourself out of the story and putting God at the center—not just saying it with our lips but truly believing it. Because when you rest in the truth that God works in you, you no longer have to chase praise.

Participants, Not Heroes

Have you ever heard someone give a report of what God is doing but try to subtly insert their name into the story? This often happens when people first come to faith in Christ—they're excited and being transformed, but you often hear about how they figured it out, and then God came along. We are experts at self-praise.

I've also seen this in mission reports. People recount amazing things they've witnessed, but they tell the stories in such a way that all you hear is, "Wow, that person is amazing." But listen—in the end, we are just participants. God deserves all the credit because he is the one who transforms hearts and lives.

There is something incredibly freeing about knowing God did it.

Reflection

We're so quick to stand at the center of our own stories, collecting applause for the victories only God can win. Where might you be tempted to cast yourself as the hero, and how can you instead point the spotlight back to him?

DAY 55

SPIRIT-EMPOWERED COURAGE

ACTS 22

"Brothers and fathers, listen now to my defense." (22:1)

YOU'VE SEEN it before—how a rowdy crowd's collective IQ seems to drop by about thirty points. Maybe you've been at a sporting event where people react to a referee's call they can't even see, and suddenly everyone is booing the ref. Or maybe you've seen panic break out in a large group setting, and it spreads like wildfire.

Paul faces a hostile audience in Jerusalem. The crowd has already beat him. The Roman soldiers have arrested him to save his life. But Paul, instead of going with the soldiers, turns to the soldiers and asks if he could be allowed to speak to the very people who wanted him dead. What courage!

He stands and speaks to them in Aramaic, trying to connect with them over common language. He shares his background and personal story to try to lay some common ground. But then he says things that are deeply offensive to their ears—the truth that Jesus is the Messiah and the Gentiles are equal heirs of the promises of God.

Today's culture seems to equate courage with writing strongly worded posts on social media. People applaud, saying, "Wow, you're so brave for taking that stand!" But is that true courage?

Some think courage means denouncing others, as if love is defined by destroying someone else's argument.

Paul is certainly offensive in his words, but his courage isn't confined to closed doors or hidden in the shadows. It isn't rooted in condemning others. He doesn't attack any of the people personally. His heart is shaped by love—remember Romans 9: He wished he could be cut off from Christ for the sake of his fellow Israelites. Love, not anger, drives Paul to speak.

Courage exists because there's something to overcome. Talking to people who have tried to kill you takes courage because fear is natural in such situations. It takes courage to tell the truth, especially when it's difficult. But Paul's courage isn't just about boldness; it is about love for the very people who are trying to hurt him. Jesus promises that his servants will receive words from the Holy Spirit for situations just like this (Luke 12:11–12). Supernatural help is necessary.

I think we often confuse courage with anger, slander, or the absence of fear. True courage, though, comes from something far greater—something that has taken over Paul's life. This courage empowers him by the Holy Spirit to obediently and compassionately speak the truth. How might you ask the Spirit to give you compassionate courage?

Love in the Face of Fury

When Jan, an Afghan refugee, became a Christian, his entire life was transformed. He was afraid to tell his family, unsure of how they would react. But the change in his demeanor was unmistakable, and soon his family noticed. They grew curious, wondering why Jan's emotions had shifted so dramatically.

One day, Jan's brother confronted him directly, asking, "Why are you so happy?" Fear surged through Jan. He knew that if he revealed his Christian faith, his brother might kill him. Desperately, he prayed for guidance. Then, feeling prompted, he asked,

"What do you think love is?" His brother responded, "I love my wife." Jan pressed further: "No, not who do you love—but what is love?" Caught off guard, his brother admitted, "I don't know."

Jan gently began reciting Paul's words from 1 Corinthians 13, "Do you think love is patient, kind, not proud?" His brother fell silent, listening. Then, after a moment, he quietly said, "Yeah, you're right."

Weeks passed. Then one day, his brother returned—this time, with fire in his eyes, seething with anger. "That definition of love you gave me—it's from the Bible!" he shouted. "Do you read this book? Do you believe this book? Are you a Christian?"

Fear gripped Jan again. He shot up a quick prayer and, feeling a quiet prompting, simply asked, "Do you agree with it?"

His brother's fury slowly faded. His breathing steadied, and he stood there, speechless, staring at Jan. After a long, tense minute, he turned and left without saying a word.

Reflection

Paul's courage in facing an angry crowd wasn't fueled by outrage or the need to prove himself right—it was rooted in a Christlike love that willingly risked rejection for the sake of others. Where might God be calling you to speak truth in love, even when it comes at a cost?

DAY 56
WAITING
ACTS 23:11; 24:27

The following night the Lord stood near Paul and said, "Take courage! As you have testified about me in Jerusalem, so you must also testify in Rome." (23:11)

When two years had passed . . . . (24:27)

ACTS 21 occurred in AD 57 and Acts 27 in AD 59.

Those two long years are filled with trials, defenses, and legal battles, but they are also marked by a significant absence: no conversions, no miracles, and no breakthroughs. There is no angel to break Paul out of jail. There is no demon to confront. There is no person to be healed.

Think about that—two years of waiting, not knowing exactly when or how God's promise will be fulfilled.

Paul knows he is destined for Rome, but the journey to that promise is filled with delays and uncertainties. For two years, Paul sits in a Roman prison, making his defense to rulers, waiting for the legal system to make a move, and trusting that God is still in control. It's so long, that it seems the Jewish opponents who threatened to kill him have forgotten him.

God is orchestrating events that will eventually take Paul to the very heart of the Roman Empire, where the gospel will be proclaimed in ways no one could have foreseen. In Acts 27, as Paul finally boards the ship to Rome, it feels like the journey is moving again. But the two years of waiting are part of God's plan too. The God who breaks Paul out of jail in Philippi also leaves him in jail in Jerusalem for two years. Why?

Waiting can feel like inactivity, like wasted time. For two years, Paul waits. From an outsider's perspective, it might seem like his ministry has stalled, like the promises of God are delayed indefinitely. But God's timing is not ours. Instead, God is working in our waiting. Have you ever had a season of waiting? If you are wondering whether God has forgotten you amid a hard season of life, consider that Paul sits in Jerusalem for two years after healing the sick, escaping from prisons, raising the dead, and bringing the gospel to the Roman world.

Waiting is Never Wasted

After Fernanda came to Christ, she labored in prayer for four years for her husband's salvation. She prayed and fasted relentlessly, making his salvation a regular prayer request shared in her discipleship group, small groups, and church retreats. Many in the church were praying regularly for her spiritist husband and even meeting with him.

Yet, for four years, nothing changed.

Then, after years of prayer, a small shift occurred. He began waiting in the car with the window down after dropping her and the kids off at church. Since the church building was open-air, he could hear the service from his car. A few months later, he began walking them inside but would wait outside for the service to end. Still, he was listening.

From there, you can imagine the progression. He moved from standing at the back to eventually sitting with her during the service. Finally, he surrendered his life to Christ.

Paul waits two years; Fernanda waited four. God is not bound by our timetables, but his timing is always perfect.

Reflection

Paul's two-year wait in prison reminds us that God's plans often unfold in the quiet stretch of time when nothing seems to be happening. And yet, Paul holds fast to what he knows: God made a promise. The destination hasn't changed, even if the pace has. While Paul waits, sometimes in chains, God is working. The same God who once broke Paul out of jail now leaves him in jail—and he is just as faithful in both.

Have you ever felt forgotten in a season like that? Maybe you've prayed for years with no response. Perhaps your suffering has lingered longer than expected. Maybe your calling feels stalled, your dreams shelved, your momentum gone. But if Paul's story teaches us anything, it's that waiting is not wasted. Those two years were not a pause in Paul's mission—they were part of it.

God's silence is never abandonment. His delays are not denials. His timing, though often confusing, is always perfect.

DAY 57

FRIENDS FOR THE BOAT RIDE

ACTS 27:1–2

When it was decided that we would sail for Italy, Paul and some other prisoners were handed over to a centurion named Julius, who belonged to the Imperial Regiment. We boarded a ship from Adramyttium about to sail for ports along the coast of the province of Asia, and we put out to sea. Aristarchus, a Macedonian from Thessalonica, was with us.

AS SUFFERING comes into your life, do you have friends you can turn to? Friends who wouldn't feel ashamed to stand by you, even in your weakest moments? Our need for community is clear from the earliest accounts of the church. Here we see the role true friends play in Paul's hardship.

Acts 27 details Paul's traveling companions as he sets off for Italy —Luke and Aristarchus. How are they allowed on the boat? We know this was a ship for prisoners and soldiers, so most likely, Luke and Aristarchus have to pay for their own passage. Here are two friends who are willing to accompany Paul, the prisoner, even when it costs them something. They stick with him. Why is that important? Because it's easy to support someone for a short time, especially when things are exciting. But as things drag on, become monotonous, or grow difficult, the enthusiasm fades, and many drop out. Think about how Bible study groups often shrink as the weeks go by.

Paul has been in jail for two years. We don't know what happens during this time. Days, weeks, and months pass between his defenses and trials. Yet, Luke and Aristarchus stick with him. They must be waiting around Jerusalem for months, unsure of when Paul's journey will begin. And when the time comes, they go with him.

The second group is the Christians in Sidon. Paul gets to visit friends, but not to teach or encourage them this time. Instead, they minister to him. They provide for his needs. This is a beautiful example of hospitality. It's important to see Paul the human being here. This is Paul the sufferer, Paul in chains, Paul who is in pain. When he lands in Sidon, he is allowed to see friends, and he doesn't hide from them. It would have been easy to withdraw in shame, not wanting others to see the mighty apostle as a prisoner. Think about it: How many of us would want to see friends when we're physically suffering, broken, or in chains?

Paul needs friends for his journey. His suffering isn't something he endures in isolation. Some friends stick with him long-term, like Luke and Aristarchus. Others, like the Christians in Sidon, help him in the moment.

You have probably read the statistics about how lonely people are today. You might feel isolated yourself. What steps could you take to cultivate the type of friendship Paul had with others? It's easy to be with someone when they're leading the charge for Christ, when they're performing miracles, or when everything is going well. But can you be with someone when they're alone in prison, with no recognition or status to offer in return?

Serving For the Long Haul Is Not Easy

Relationships take time, and much of the missionary enterprise is built on speed. There are many reasons why most missionaries don't last more than three years and why short-term trips are so popular. Lasting ministry requires deep friendships.

In the 1960s, several missionaries were kicked out of the Congo and ended up in French-speaking Canada. Québec was a hard place to serve, and not one missionary lasted for more than six months. Tom Carson, a pastor in Québec at the time explains why:

> You have to understand that they have been used to serving in a part of the world where they have seen much blessing. They are used to considerable crowds, they have built clinics and hospitals, they have seen many people converted and helped to train pastors to teach them. Then they arrive here and find everything to be interminably slow. How are they likely to read this, except to conclude that they must have misunderstood their call to Québec since no fruit seems to be forthcoming?[12]

People will often bail when things get slow. Paul has been out of sight for two years. And there doesn't seem to be any fruit. Consider how quickly you might jump to another church if things slow down. Or how fast you might drop a missionary whose work just isn't bearing fruit at the speed you would like.

Reflection

Just as Paul needs both steadfast companions like Luke and Aristarchus and the hospitality of Christians in Sidon, we too thrive when we allow others to stand with us in our weakest moments. Who might God be calling you to stand with—even when the journey grows long and the fruit is slow in coming?

DAY 58

THE GOSPEL UNCHAINED

ACTS 28:16

When we got to Rome, Paul was allowed to live by himself, with a soldier to guard him.

THROUGHOUT ACTS, people encounter the God of the universe through the witness of his servants. Many times, God uses a very hard circumstance in the lives of his people to bring the gospel to unexpected places.

Paul has made it to Rome and is put under house arrest. What do you think happens to all the guards who guard Paul over a two-year period? They rotate in shifts, likely dozens of different men, if not more. These soldiers aren't just guarding any prisoner—they are confined to close quarters with Paul. There is no escape, no chance to tune him out. They are a captive audience, and Paul seizes the opportunity.

Paul reflects on this in Philippians 1:12–13:

> Now I want you to know, brothers and sisters, that what has happened to me has actually served to advance the gospel. As a result, it has become clear throughout the whole palace guard and to everyone else that I am in chains for Christ.

The soldiers have seen countless prisoners before. But have they ever encountered anyone like Paul? What do you think Paul talks about during those long hours chained to a guard? These soldiers aren't just bystanders—they hear every conversation Paul has, witness every interaction. When people visit Paul, they hear deep theological discussions, encouraging words, and even dictations that would later become part of the New Testament. They hear Paul speak about the risen Christ, the transforming power of the gospel, and the hope of eternal life.

Paul's joy, even in chains, must baffle them. Most prisoners would be desperate, complaining, or defeated. Not Paul. He writes letters filled with commands for joy, words of encouragement, and instructions on living a life of faith. He speaks of contentment in all circumstances. And these soldiers, who watch his every move, see it lived out in real time.

Think about the ripple effect. These soldiers, after their time guarding Paul, were eventually reassigned or deployed to different regions across the Roman Empire. They carry with them not only the memory of their time with Paul but also the seed of the gospel planted in their hearts. The gospel is spreading, even through Paul's imprisonment.

Why? Because Paul is in chains, and he is chained to them. And as a result, the gospel spreads to the military.

God's strategy of spreading the gospel from a prison cell is yet another example of the unexpected ways God works to spread the gospel. Can you recall a time God's work may seemed to have been stopped, only to see him use a hard situation for the further spreading of his gospel?

Unstoppable Good News

Twenty years ago, my Iranian friend was watching satellite TV when the remote fell on the floor and changed the station to a pirated Christian channel. It was the first time he heard about Jesus. A few years later he left Iran and came to Europe, where he met Christians who shared the gospel with him. It was the love of God that eventually drew him to Christ.

Today, he pastors a church that has seen thousands of Iranians come to Christ. The ripple effects of a remote falling on the floor and a pirated Christian channel are felt throughout all of Europe today, as many of these Iranians have spread out and shared the gospel there.

Reflection

Pray for eyes to see unexpected opportunities. Ask God to help you see the "house arrest" moments in your life—difficult situations or unwanted detours—as opportunities for gospel witness. Pray that even small seeds planted through your life would grow far beyond what you can see—just as the soldiers who guarded Paul carried the gospel across the Roman Empire.

DAY 59

BEAUTY FROM SUFFERING

ACTS 28:30–31

For two whole years Paul stayed there in his own rented house and welcomed all who came to see him. He proclaimed the kingdom of God and taught about the Lord Jesus Christ—with all boldness and without hindrance!

WHAT ELSE does Paul do while in Rome? He writes. Ephesians, Philippians, Colossians, and Philemon. Those letters hit you differently when you realize where he is writing from. His letters are filled with joy. They are filled with peace. He is not moping around. Don't you think he should have been prone to despair? After all, he sees Nero's palace. He is under house arrest. His ministry seems over.

As you get older and you experience life, you may not stay as optimistic as you used to be. The hardships of life can really crush you. Yet here is Paul, in chains for nearly five years, inviting over his enemies, and talking to anyone who will visit.

Consider the verses we get from prison:

> What is more, I consider everything a loss because of the surpassing worth of knowing Christ Jesus my Lord, for whose sake I have lost all things. I consider them garbage, that I may gain Christ. (Philippians 3:8)

> I can do all this through him who gives me strength. (Philippians 4:13)
>
> For it is by grace you have been saved, through faith—and this is not from yourselves, it is the gift of God—not by works, so that no one can boast. (Ephesians 2:8–9)
>
> As a prisoner for the Lord, then, I urge you to live a life worthy of the calling you have received. (Ephesians 4:1)
>
> Be kind and compassionate to one another, forgiving each other, just as in Christ God forgave you. (Ephesians 4:32)

For many Christians, their favorite verses in the Bible come from these letters. Don't all of those passages strike you with a deeper meaning when you realize where Paul is writing from? The man is writing this from prison, waiting to testify before Caesar. You can imagine how Satan must be so thrilled that Paul is in chains. He may think he shut down Paul and his influence. But surprise! God's good plans are not thwarted. Not only does Paul continue to boldly proclaim the gospel to all he encounters, but he also devotes himself to equipping and encouraging the churches he has helped to start. These letters, written from the worst of circumstances, give the entire global church the gift of Ephesians, Philippians, Colossians, Philemon, 1 and 2 Timothy, Titus, and Philemon.

And from the shadow of Nero's golden palace, what does he write? That one day every knee will bow and every tongue acknowledge that Jesus Christ is Lord (Philippians 2:10–11). Paul isn't writing these words disconnected from reality. He is writing these words chained to guards who had once said "Caesar is Lord" but now say, "Jesus is Lord."

How do the words of Paul in his letters hit you now that you know he wrote them from prison? How might it adjust your expectations of the Christian life, and how might you respond differently to the hard situations you find yourself in? How can you use those situations to proclaim the kingdom of God?

Powerful Prison Letters

My Afghan friend came to Christ in part because of the letters Paul wrote from prison. He recounted going to a mosque, and when he asked for a copy of the Quran, he was told he had to pay for it. He then went to a church and they offered him a Bible for free. He read the Bible, including the words Paul wrote from prison, and was saved.

I once met two migrant women who came to know the Lord when a smuggler handed them a Bible and told them to pretend they were Christians to get asylum. Instead, the women read the Bible, and what the smuggler meant for evil, God turned for good. They read Paul's words and were saved.

Paul was locked up for the gospel, and the Word of the Lord continues to spread—across cultures, across socioeconomic barriers, and across the centuries. Two thousand years later, an Afghan Muslim read what Paul wrote and trusted Christ.

Reflection

Paul's prison letters remind us that the Christian life isn't lived in idyllic circumstances. Paul's attitude toward his time in prison seems dominated by joy and contentment despite hard circumstances. When you are alone or suffering, how might you use those times in your life to grow in trusting the Lord, rather than giving in to despair?

DAY 60

THE UNFINISHED STORY

ACTS 28:31

He proclaimed the kingdom of God
and taught about the Lord Jesus Christ—
with all boldness and without hindrance!

PAUL IS in prison. Nero is on his throne. The number of Jesus followers around the world seems minuscule compared to the number of those perishing without Christ. And so ends the book of Acts. Does it end on a high note or in defeat?

Luke ends the book of Acts mid-motion, in a way that invites us to continue the story. Though the narrative of Acts concludes, the mission of God does not. The gospel message moves forward unhindered all the way to today. We are part of that ongoing story. The narrative is not centered on Paul; it's about the Holy Spirit working through God's people to testify about Jesus Christ, the risen Messiah.

Today, we are living witnesses to this same kingdom of God and the Lord Jesus. The story that begins with the apostles now continues through us. We are caught up in the grand narrative of God's redemptive work, a story that seeks to make sense of this world. The kingdom of God breaks into history with the coming of the Christ, as God plants his feet on creation to reclaim it for himself. This Messiah is Jesus, who has been drawing people into his kingdom for over two thousand years.

Acts 28 is not the final chapter of God's work in the world. And this is why I tell stories from everywhere. God is at work. God is planting churches in the Middle East. God is with my friends in jail in Myanmar. God is with his people in Bhutan, and Nigeria, and Ghana, and Cameroon. And God is at work in Lincoln, Nebraska, and Sacramento, California, and Odessa, Texas, and Bozeman, Montana. He is weaving together a tapestry of stories that are all signposts pointing right at him.

I tell these stories to drive a theological point home—that the Lord is redeeming people from every tribe and nation. They are modern-day, visual reminders of what you read about in Scripture.

Like the Israelites, we so easily forget what God has done. We need to be reminded of his work in the world. How have these stories changed your view of the church and of what God is doing around the world? Take time to thank God for the work he is accomplishing through his people.

Taking Up the Mission

In 1999, Wycliffe Bible Translators and SIL International recognized that at the current pace of Bible translation, it would take until the year 2150 for every people group on earth to have God's Word in their own language. With so many people groups still without a Bible in their native tongue, it became clear that a new strategy was needed.

Rather than relying solely on foreign workers, local churches have begun to take up the work of translation themselves. For example, the FJKM Church in Madagascar mobilized three hundred volunteers to translate the Bible from the national Malagasy language into various local languages. As a result of this grassroots effort, four New Testament translations have been completed in just five years, and four more are on their way.

SIL International has also observed a significant shift: A 20 percent decrease in foreign workers has been matched by a

70 percent increase in indigenous translators, demonstrating that the global church is actively stepping up to reach those geographically and culturally close to them.

For the first time in history, the leadership of four key Bible agencies—SIL International, United Bible Societies, Wycliffe Global Alliance, and The Word for the World—are all led by individuals from the continent of Africa. This unprecedented change reflects the global church's growing ownership and leadership in the mission of Bible translation.

The gospel is moving forward. God's kingdom is advancing. And the global church is rising together to bring the good news to every corner of the world.

Reflection

The abrupt ending of Acts reminds us that God's work in the world is still unfolding—that our own stories are chapters in this continuing gospel narrative. Across continents and cultures, believers are stepping into that mission, proving that God's kingdom never stalls, no matter who sits on any earthly throne. Where and how might God be calling you to join this ever-advancing story of redemption today?

ACKNOWLEDGMENTS

NO BOOK comes into existence without the generous support and encouragement of many people. My journey into missions began with a brief but significant conversation with Hutz Hertzberg, was deepened through a transformative missions class with Jim Plueddemann, and took shape years later with a pitch to Tom Steller and John Piper to launch a missions organization at Bethlehem Baptist Church. They took a leap of faith with me—even though I'd never been overseas! As John once remarked, "Let's just let it happen and see what happens." That initial trust now feels like ancient history, but without their confidence and courage, I would never have experienced firsthand the incredible ways God is moving around the globe.

I have personally witnessed extraordinary grace in being granted a front-row seat to God's global mission, even while knowing that I see only the smallest fraction of his work. The true heroes are the people whose stories fill these pages. Many of them are now my friends. As I wrote these stories, it made me long to be able to be with you. One day I will.

This book became a reality because Champ Thornton encouraged me, Stephen Witmer—in God's timing—made a key introduction, Brad Byrd pressed this thing forward, and the wonderful team at New Growth Press believed in the potential of a missions-focused devotional. Special thanks go to Barbara Juliani and Ruth Castle, whose insightful input and thoughtful engagement significantly improved these devotions.

To the board and staff at Training Leaders International: I deeply love and admire each of you. Our shared ministry is profoundly important, and while we set out to serve and pour ourselves out for the global church, we often return home with our own cups overflowing.

To Redeemer Church of Bozeman, thank you for your faithful and loving support. It is a joy and privilege to serve as one of your pastors and to invite you into the story that God continues to weave across the world.

Amy, I love you deeply, sweetheart.

Finally, this book is dedicated to my five loud, fun, joyful, energetic, musical, theatrical children. You've grown up with a father who travels the globe for the sake of the gospel, bearing costs you did not have any choice in. My continual prayer is that your hearts would deeply cherish the gospel and that your eyes would be opened to the beauty and brokenness of the world around you. I'm profoundly grateful and proud to be your dad.

ENDNOTES

1. "2024 Global Scripture Access." Wycliffe Global Alliance, December 11, 2024, https://www.wycliffe.net/resources/statistics/.

2. Eugene H. Peterson, *Answering God: The Psalms as Tools for Prayer* (HarperOne, 1992), 12.

3. Eifion Evans, *The Welsh Revival of 1904* (Bridgend, 1969), 70.

4. John R. W. Stott, *The Message of Acts: The Spirit, the Church, & the World* (Downers Grove, IL: InterVarsity Press, 1990), 100.

5. Bulletin announcement in Glenn Schwartz, "Two Awesome Problems: How Short-Term Missions Can Go Wrong," *International Journal of Frontier Missions* 20, no. 4 (2004): 33.

6. Tom Steller, "The Ola Hanson Story | Bethlehem Baptist Church," accessed May 8, 2025, https://bethlehem.church/the-ola-hanson-story/.

7. William Barclay, "Commentary on Acts 11," William Barclay's Daily Study Bible, https://www.studylight.org/commentaries/eng/dsb/acts-11.html, 1956–59.

8. John Newton, quoted in John Stott, *Acts: Seeing the Spirit at Work* (InterVarsity Press, 2008), 67.

9. World Missionary Conference, 1910. *The History and Records of the Conference Together with Addresses Delivered at the Evening Meetings* (Revell: New York, 1910), 315, https://www.rasmusen.org/special/Azariah.1910.pdf.

10. Tim Keller (@timkellernyc), Health Update: Today, Dad is being discharged from the hospital to receive hospice care at home. Twitter, May 18, 2023, https://x.com/timkellernyc/status/1659314127125225479.

11. Grace Scott, *Twenty-Six Years of Missionary Work in China* (American Tract Society, 1897), 3.

12. D. A. Carson, *Memoirs of an Ordinary* Pastor (Crossway, 2008), 77.